# Indoor Plants

**Brian Ward and
Tom Wellsted**

**Macdonald Guidelines**

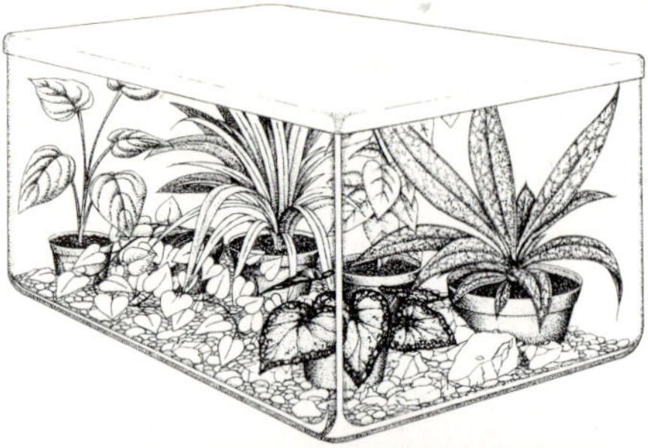

© Macdonald Educational Ltd
1977

First published 1977
Macdonald Educational Ltd
Holywell House
Worship Street
London EC2A 2EN

Printed and bound by
Waterlow (Dunstable)
Limited

**ISBN 0 356 06017 9**

# Contents

# What is an indoor plant?

Of the hundreds of thousands of species of plants occurring throughout the world, a select few have been chosen to share our homes. Other home plants have been selectively bred and propagated, picking out those that thrive in the unnatural conditions of the home, and improving their hardiness and appearance.

The plants commonly offered in florists and nursery centres as 'indoor plants' vary from desert cacti, through creeping jungle vines, to young forms of trees from sub-tropical forests. If you are going to keep them successfully, quite obviously you will need to be aware of the special requirements of these plants, as the part of your home in which you place them must approximate as closely as is practicable to their natural habitats.

The enormous variety of cultivated indoor plants means that you can select suitable plants for absolutely any home. You might need a large, stately plant for your hallway, trailing plants to decorate a wall, tiny cacti for a narrow windowsill, or flowering bulbs which will enjoy only a temporary stay indoors before being relegated to the garden.

All can be classed as 'indoor plants', although those grown purely as foliage plants are more usually termed 'house plants'. Bulbs and flowering shrubs like azaleas and fuchsias have been grown indoors for many years, while even earlier types of indoor plants were popularized by the Victorians—ferns, palms, and the legendary aspidistra. The modern 'house plants' made their appearance after World War II, with the realization that more exotic plants did not need to be permanently kept in the heated greenhouse. The advent of centrally-heated homes, well-lit rooms and the better insulation and draught-proofing of the modern home meant that many of these delicate plants could now tolerate the indoor environment.

## The naming of plants

Throughout the English-speaking world, a few plant names are universally recognized: the Rubber Plant, ivies, ferns, and several more besides. But what are we to make of the Swiss Cheese Plant, or Mexican Breadfruit? These are popular names of the large indoor plant with perforated leaves, botanically known as *Monstera deliciosa*. Such an unwieldy name, based on Latin (or sometimes Greek), has one tremendous advantage over the popular name; it is universally recognized by growers, nurserymen and florists, and is generally unambiguous. In any country in the world, horticulturists use this same name for the identical plant. For this reason, botanical names for indoor plants are used throughout this book. Once you are familiar with these names, you will be able to use them to identify related but less familiar plants.

The first part of the name is called the 'generic' name. *Ficus*, for example, is a genus of trees and shrubs which, to the botanist, can be grouped together because of the similar structures of their flowers and internal parts, although to our eyes they may appear wildly dissimilar. The second part of the name describes the actual species, such as *Ficus elastica*, the common Rubber Plant. Other species are *Ficus benjamina*, a graceful weeping shrub, and *Ficus pumila*, a dainty vine-like plant looking nothing like the well-known Rubber Plant.

◄ Growing wild in the Canaries, the geranium (*Pelargonium*) and Prickly Pear (*Opuntia*). These are now familiar indoor plants readily available from florists and garden centres.

If a small 'x' appears before the second part, it means that the plant is a hybrid.

Sometimes you will find another name added to the two basic botanical names. 'Variegata', for instance, means that this plant is a variegated variety with alternating light-coloured and darker-green foliage. Quite often, the third name appears in quotation marks, and is obviously not latinized; this shows that the plant is a variety developed under cultivation, and is not a natural freak or mutation which has developed in the wild. Most of the spectacular flowering indoor plants are cultivated varieties, or cultivars, as they are more correctly known.

Unfortunately, in a few cases the botanical names cause added confusion, as occasionally the botanists decide that their classifications need adjustment. Hence a plant once well known as *Dracaena indivisa*, with long and attractive strap-shaped leaves, may also be found labelled as *Cordyline indivisa* or, in its latest form, *C. australis* (the generic name is generally shortened to an initial letter after the first reference to the plant).

## The indoor gardener

Many people presented with an indoor plant, or buying one as a table decoration at Christmas, are content to enjoy its attractive appearance for a while, discarding it as soon as it appears to have lost its initial healthy appearance. A healthy indoor plant is an asset to any home, but a sick plant is an unpleasant sight, and often a very expensive one, if you own one of the more ornamental species.

Once you have found the best place in your home for the type of plant you have, there is no reason why, with a little care and understanding, you should not be able to enjoy it for many years. You will probably be able to propagate other plants from it; you will certainly know how to look after related plants, after the lessons you have learned. One of the best things about keeping indoor plants is that you can generally learn from experience without killing the plant, as if conditions are not to its liking it will respond by looking generally unhealthy, rather than by promptly expiring. You should have adequate time to notice

The Wardian case was a sealed box, originally used by Victorian plant-collectors to bring home their delicate discoveries from the tropics. In this closed environment even the most delicate ferns thrived and their culture became a craze. Ornate fern cases, made from wrought iron, and covered with attractive glass domes, were soon a feature of the fashionable Victorian drawing room. Some of these are now valuable antiques.

◀ Another popular 19th century introduction was the palm, which was able to survive in the draughty, chilly, and often poorly-lit Victorian home. Large specimens were especially valued, and were able to grow to a good size, due partly to the high ceilings of homes built at that time. The aspidistra was another popular indoor plant, being extremely hardy and tolerant of the worst growing conditions.

the plant's plight, and rectify the situation.

Ideally, you will not find yourself saddled with an unsuitable inhabitant for your living-room. Instead, you will have decided in advance of your purchase exactly what you need to improve the appearance of the room. The room conditions, and the position in which the plant will stand, should determine the type of plant you will buy.

The last section of this book contains details of many of the popular indoor plants, together with notes on their cultivation, and their needs and preferences. But when you go into a nursery or garden centre, you will be confronted with many more types of indoor plant, some probably quite unfamiliar. Some of these are unsuitable for indoor cultivation, thriving only in a heated greenhouse, and surviving reluctantly for a short while when brought into the home. Ask for advice if you are doubtful whether such plants are right for you—sometimes a novel plant is a hardy recent introduction. Others sell well for a short time, then vanish from the shops and nurseries when it is realized that they are unsuitable for home cultivation.

Even with these limitations on your choice, there are many hundreds of exotic plants you can raise in your home. In a bottle garden or in a fern case the most delicate plants can be grown in the ordinary living-room. For those with sufficient patience, the Japanese art of bonsai can be tried, producing tiny gnarled trees which look hundreds of years old, and may actually take 20 years or more to reach a reasonable size.

When you have mastered the art of indoor gardening, there are even more demanding variations to try. By using specially-designed fluorescent lights, flowering plants can be raised out of season in the darkest rooms, and will often produce specimens even more perfect than those grown in greenhouses. Indoor plants can also be grown without soil, by hydroponics —a process where the roots are bedded in an inert gravel soaked in water containing artificially added nutrients.

By such techniques you can adjust and manipulate the environment in which your plants grow, in order to get the best from them.

## IN THE WILD

Indoor plants come from an enormous variety of natural habitats. Plants cultivated from tropical and sub-tropical species, such as cacti and succulents, seem to do best in the warmth of the home, provided adequate humidity can be maintained. In general, plants from temperate climates and mountainous regions do less well indoors, tending to 'bolt' if kept permanently in the home. They are best grown outdoors for most of the year, being brought in during the flowering period.

1.   Rhododendrons
2.   *Camellia japonica*
3.   Rhododendrons
4–7. Narcissi
8.   Cyclamen
9.   Crocus
10.  *Lithops*
11.  *Notocactus ottonis*
12.  *Echinocereus*

Mountains and Foothills

Temperate Zone

Desert

Scrub

Swamp

Semi tropi

**Tropical**

9

# How a plant works

Simple though it appears, a plant can carry out most of the functions we associate with more complex forms of life, such as mammals. Using only simple foods, a plant can grow and reproduce itself, although the extent to which it thrives will depend on the ready availability of the foods and habitats it needs. The indoor plant is a 'captive', totally dependent on its owner to provide all the necessities for healthy life.

The basic processes of life in the plant depend on the availability of water and suitable food substances in the soil, oxygen and carbon dioxide in the air, and adequate light. In the leaves, these ingredients are combined by the process of photosynthesis, which produces sugar, the plant's food. Leaves are complicated organs developed in a way that allows photosynthesis to be carried out most effectively. Most leaves are flattened, and are positioned so that they face the sun or, if in the shade, grow so as to face the direction from which most light comes.

This positioning of the leaves means that they are able to take in the maximum amount of light, which, with the aid of the green pigment chlorophyll, 'powers' the whole process of photosynthesis. Plants growing naturally in shaded areas such as the *Philodendron* family, *Monstera*, *Ficus*, and many of the other familiar indoor plants, have large leaves to take advantage of all the light they can get. Plants which naturally experience a surfeit of sun, growing in deserts or other exposed areas, have no need of such extensive leaf systems, and their leaves are often reduced to sparse spines or needles. Leaves may even be absent altogether, as in cacti, where photosynthesis takes place in the stems.

## Habitat

The shape of a plant is also affected by its habitat. *Ficus elastica*, the Rubber Plant, is obviously well shaped to shoot up through surrounding vegetation in order to reach the light. Ivies and climbing philodendrons reach the light by swarming up any convenient tree-trunk. Ground-living ferns, on the other hand, make the most of what light is available below the trees by means of their finely divided leaves, which increase the area available for photosynthesis.

The general structure of a plant is determined by its ancestry, but its actual shape when grown indoors depends on the environment you provide. Too little light, or too few nutrients, and your plant will be leggy and delicate, or stunted and discoloured.

## The flower

Although all plants have the same basic design, they are extensively modified to suit differing habitats and life-styles. Nowhere is this specialization more marked than in the flower, which is intended solely as an organ of reproduction. The plant's objective is to get pollen from the stamens of the same, or another flower, onto its stigma, where it will start the process of fertilization which culminates in seed production. Many plants rely on insects to carry the pollen, and to attract them plants have evolved bright colours and powerful scents. The shape of the flower may also be modified to assist insect pollination, forcing bees and other insects to crawl over the exposed pollen as they feed on nectar produced within the flower.

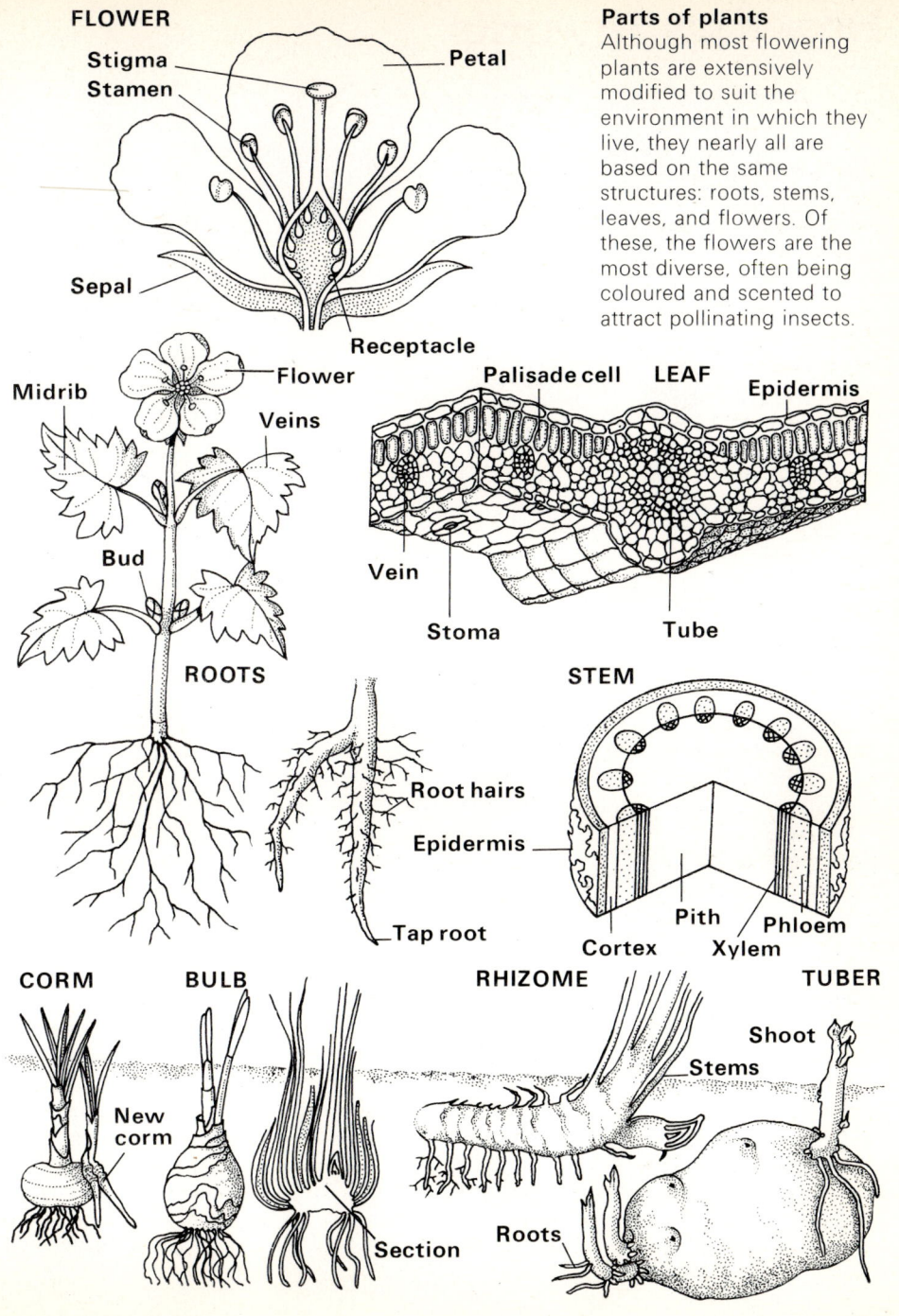

# FLOWER

Stigma
Stamen
Petal
Sepal
Receptacle

## Parts of plants
Although most flowering plants are extensively modified to suit the environment in which they live, they nearly all are based on the same structures: roots, stems, leaves, and flowers. Of these, the flowers are the most diverse, often being coloured and scented to attract pollinating insects.

Midrib
Flower
Veins
Bud

## LEAF
Palisade cell
Epidermis
Vein
Stoma
Tube

## ROOTS
Root hairs
Epidermis
Tap root

## STEM
Pith
Phloem
Cortex
Xylem

CORM
New corm

BULB
Section

RHIZOME
Stems
Roots

TUBER
Shoot

11

# HOW A PLANT WORKS

The plant is an efficient chemical factory which extracts simple nutrients from the soil and the surrounding air, building them up into the complex chemicals it needs to sustain life.

1

2

3

4

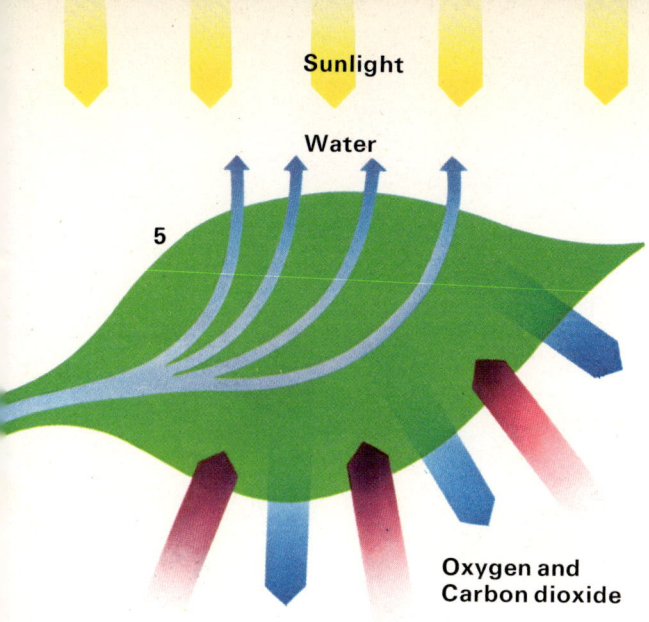

**Sunlight**

**Water**

5

**Oxygen and Carbon dioxide**

## The working parts

All living plants are built to the same basic plan, with roots, stems, and leaves, although some, like cacti, are extensively modified to allow stems to function as leaves.

**1. Root hairs** The finest division of a plant's roots. These microscopic fibres can be seen as a delicate fluff on plant roots which grow through the drain holes of the pot. In the compost, these tiny root hairs grow around the individual grains of the soil. Soil particles are surrounded by a film of water, containing dissolved nutrients: potassium, phosphorus and nitrogen, as well as many equally important trace elements which the plant uses in small quantities. These substances, and the water in which they are dissolved, are absorbed by the root hairs and passed on to the root system proper.

**2. The roots** They collect the water and nutrients absorbed from the soil, and pass them to the rest of the plant along a series of fine tubes. They also serve to anchor the plant firmly, by spreading through the soil. In some plants, the roots act as storage organs when the rest of the plant dies off during the winter, preserving sufficient food and energy to start off the next season's growth.

**3. The stem** This serves to convey water and nutrients up from the roots to the leaves. Like the roots, it contains tubes which conduct liquid. It also contains bundles of very strong fibres which give the stem its strength, which is necessary to support the leaves and flowers and prevent wind damage. In woody-stemmed plants, the tubes become hard and thickened, producing a 'trunk', and a corky bark protects the outer layers.

**4. Small branches or petioles** These connect the leaves to the stem and have a similar type of structure to stems, but do not need to be so strong.

**5. The leaf** The key to the plant's whole life. It contains chlorophyll, a green pigment. In sunlight, this reacts with water brought up from the roots, and carbon dioxide from the air, to produce sugar, the plant's food. Oxygen is given off as a waste product. At night, oxygen is absorbed to help break down the sugar and release the energy needed for growth, while carbon dioxide is liberated. This endless cycle powers the whole plant. On the underside of the leaves are stomata: tiny openings which can open or shut as required. Water constantly evaporates through these, causing a 'suction' which draws more water up from the roots. If conditions are too hot these stomata close up, reducing the rate of evaporation to protect the plant. The upper surface of the leaf is covered with a protective waxy cuticle.

# Types of plants

With a little care, you can grow representatives of just about every type of higher plant in the home, the exceptions being the primitive forms like algae—the seaweeds and the slimy blanket-weed which forms in ponds. All plants are modified in some way in order to suit a particular environment, and the more advanced types of plants have developed structural modifications which allow them to cope with a large range of habitats. This also means that the primitive plants are much more sensitive to alterations in their environment, as they lack the specialized organs necessary to cope with changes in humidity, light intensity and temperature.

One such plant is selaginella, a pretty creeping plant not much more evolved than the mosses, and often used in indoor garden display troughs. Its delicate lacy foliage cannot long survive the dry atmosphere in the home, and soon becomes scorched. Unless it can be kept in a shaded greenhouse it is best raised in a bottle garden, where the high humidity and subdued lighting provide adequate protection.

## Ferns

Ferns are among the oldest types of plants known, and the imprints of their lacy fronds are often found in lumps of coal. They are also among the earliest types of house plant, and they became something of a craze with the Victorians. As primitive plants, ferns produce no seeds, but grow from dust-like spores produced on the underside of their fronds. They do not possess the water-retaining organs of the higher plants, and are easily scorched by dry air. Some ferns are tough enough for indoor cultivation, but those especially coveted by the Victorian collectors were so delicate that they could be severely damaged by even a few minutes' exposure to dry air. The secret of their cultivation was the Wardian case, a sealed, glass-sided box in which temperature and humidity could be strictly controlled. These containers were originally developed so that botanists could bring newly discovered ferns home without having them die off on a long sea voyage, but they were soon transformed into highly decorative centre-pieces for the Victorian drawing-room. The rare and temperamental species most valued by the Victorians have long been discarded for indoor cultivation, and most of those now available are quite hardy and easy to grow. However, because of their ancestry and

To cope with the desert environment, cacti and succulents have become fantastically modified. Their leaves are reduced or absent, to reduce evaporation of precious water, and many are covered with spines or hairs, to protect them from browsing animals. Lithops, also known as Living Stones, are protected by being inconspicuous. Coloured and shaped exactly like pebbles they are almost unnoticeable, except when, for a brief while, they are covered with brilliantly-coloured flowers.

limitations, they always appreciate a moist atmosphere. If this cannot easily be provided, they will benefit from having their foliage sprayed regularly with water. Like the selaginellas, smaller species of fern thrive in the bottle garden or in up-to-date versions of the Wardian case, where their delicate pale-green foliage provides an attractive contrast to the darker leaves of most other plants.

Sometimes quite unrelated types of plant, such as various species of asparagus, are incorrectly referred to as 'ferns'. These are actually flowering plants, although their lacy foliage resembles that of the ferns. They thrive in similar conditions, as would be expected of their shape and appearance, but are in general much tougher.

## Flowering plants

All the other types of indoor plants (and most outdoor plants, apart from conifers) are classed in the huge family of 'flowering

plants'; that is, they reproduce chiefly by means of seeds produced from a flower. This may seem confusing, as in many cases you will never actually *see* a flower, still less a seed, on the foliage plants grown in the home. But the group encompasses such diverse plants as oak trees, grass and cacti; all produce flowers, though they may be inconspicuous.

In the home we grow some types purely for their flowers, but the foliage plants rarely find conditions enough to their liking to produce flowers, or else they cannot develop to their mature form in the enclosed environment.

Plants kept purely for their flowers are obviously those which find indoor conditions to their liking. Most of these are herbaceous, that is, they have soft stems supported largely by the pressure of sap within them. Probably the most useful indoors is the saintpaulia or African Violet, which is available in an almost infinite number of varieties, and in colours ranging from the original violet through reds, pinks, and white. It is one of the few plants which can be kept in flower almost continuously, thanks to careful selective breeding, which has also improved its hardiness considerably. A close relative is sinningia, more popularly but incorrectly known as the gloxinia, which is one of the most spectacular of indoor flowers.

Another flowering plant which must surely be the most popular of all is impatiens, the Busy Lizzie. Its pansy-like blooms are produced in large numbers on a healthy plant, and its rate of growth is phenomenal when conditions are to its liking. Such plants as these are permanent residents of the house, but other herbaceous plants will at best give only a few months' pleasure.

Dwarf chrysanthemums are often offered as house plants, and will produce a beautiful floral display which lasts for several

15

weeks. These are really outdoor plants which thrive best on balconies and window boxes, flowering when brought indoors after the buds form. Many of those you will find in shops and nurseries have been tricked into flowering in a convenient dwarfed size by manipulating light and food supply, and treating with chemicals which stunt growth. If you keep them outdoors and bring them back indoors for the following season's flowering, you will find you now have plants reminiscent of the ordinary garden chrysanthemum, long and leggy, and needing to be tied up for support.

Carnations, botanically known as *Dianthus*, are also available for indoor cultivation, although you really need a greenhouse to bring them to their best condition. These and many other familiar garden plants like pelargoniums or geraniums can be grown indoors for part of their annual life-cycle, although they cannot be considered true indoor plants.

## Woody perennials

A smaller number of flowering indoor plants are classed as 'woody perennials', having stems covered in bark, like trees. Most of these are shrubs, the commonest being azaleas, originally coming from the foothills of the Himalayas, in India and China. The wild species vary from large trees down to creeping 'Alpine' plants not much bigger than mosses. Indoor varieties come in an almost limitless range of colours and flower shapes and when purchased have usually been treated in such a way that they will flower around Christmas time. Because of their ancestry, azaleas do not appreciate overheated homes, and thrive outdoors during the summer.

Poinsettias, technically known as *Euphorbia pulcherrima*, are also very popular as a Christmas gift. They too are shrubs, sold in an artificially dwarfed form, and their tiny insignificant flowers are surrounded

**Types of indoor plants**
1 *Adiantum tenerum*
2 *Aglaonema crispum*
3 *Anthurium andreanum*
4 *Begonia rex*
5 *Begonia tuberhybrida*
6 *Chlorophytum comosum*
7 *Codiaeum variegatum*
8 *Coleus blumei*
9 *Cordyline terminalis*
10 *Dieffenbachia picta*
11 *Dracaena marginata*
12 *Echeveria*
13 *Echeveria multicaulis*
14 *Ficus elastica*
15 *Fittonia argyroneura*
16 *Fuchsia*
17 *Hedera canariensis*
18 *Hedera helix*
19 *Hibiscus rosa-sinensis*
20 *Monstera deliciosa*
21 *Neoregelia*
22 *Notocactus tabularis*
23 *Opuntia microdasys*
24 *Pelargonium domesticum*
25 *Philodendron scandens*
26 *Platycerium bifurcatum*
27 *Pteris tremula*
28 *Rebutia violaciflora*
29 *Rhoicissus rhomboidea*
30 *Saintpaulia ionantha*
31 *Sansevieria trifasciata*
32 *Selaginella*
33 *Sinningia speciosa*
34 *Thunbergia alata*

by rosettes of vivid red or yellow bracts, of the same shape as the leaves. Generally speaking, woody-stemmed shrubs like poinsettias which are kept for the beauty of their 'flowers' are not easy to keep indoors without constant pruning, repotting, and other special treatments. They soon become leggy and ungainly, and the trick is to continuously propagate new plants from cuttings so that the older plants can be discarded.

## Orchids

Some of the most specialized and delicate of all flowering indoor plants are the orchids. As with ferns, Victorian plant collectors were obsessed with orchids, which have always been thought of as being extremely difficult to cultivate. The appeal is not difficult to understand, for orchids are undoubtedly the most spectacular and varied of all flowering plants, occurring naturally in 28,000 or more species, with another 50,000 cultivated hybrids having been developed. The hardy types thrive in conditions rather like those enjoyed by ferns, demanding a high humidity but rather more light than ferns, but even the 'easy' species and varieties of orchid are very particular about their environment. You certainly won't be able to propagate them without specialized knowledge and equipment.

## Bulbs and corms

Orchids grow from a swollen base resembling a bulb. Some less spectacular flowering plants grow from true bulbs, and are much easier to grow. Bulbs are swollen buds which act as a food store for the plant. Daffodil, narcissus, hyacinth and crocus are too well known to need description, belonging to the hardy group of plants which can spend most of the year outdoors,

being brought in only on the point of flowering. The truly exotic bulbs, like hippeastrum and other lilies, produce blooms rivalling the orchids in colour and size. They are all the more spectacular because the flower is produced on a stem which emerges from the bulb well before the leaves. Exotic bulbs are usually pre-treated, and need only be grown in damp compost, or even in water, although water-grown bulbs will not survive to flower for another year.

Corms are also storage organs, being thickened stems rather than buds, although to the uninitiated they are all classed as 'bulbs'. From tubers are grown the many varieties of cyclamen, a pretty and popular pot plant which is not really suited for conditions in the average house, and the fleshy begonias, with spectacular flowers and attractive foliage. Other types of begonia may have ordinary fibrous roots.

## Foliage plants

There is no doubt that the easiest plants to keep as permanent inhabitants of your home are the group which although technically 'flowering plants' are grown largely for the beauty of their foliage. To this group belongs the vast majority of indoor plants, in limitless shapes and sizes. Some are actually trees which in the right conditions could grow to enormous sizes. The *Araucaria*, or Norfolk Island Pine, and *Ficus elastica* and its near relatives develop into trees over the years, but lose the attractive appearance of the juvenile plant.

The large family of palms have been kept as indoor plants for more than a hundred years, and are extremely tough and slow-growing, seldom getting too big for their environment. Several species are available, ranging from the giant chamaerops which is usually seen growing in hotel foyers, offices, and department stores, and even outdoors in the warmer parts of Britain and Europe, down to dwarf species which will not outgrow the smallest room, like rheinhardtia, the Window Palm.

A number of other plants superficially resemble palms, although they are quite unrelated. Dracaena and cordyline have palm-like leaves, often with attractive

◀ In the bottle garden, conditions remain constant throughout the year, apart from variations in light intensity. Consequently even delicate plants grow well, protected from the drying effect of the air in the modern home. However, care must be taken to choose plants which will not outgrow their environment.

variegations and stripes of white, yellow, and even bright red. They are much more attractive than true palms, but are less tolerant of dry conditions, cold and poor light. These too can grow into large shrubs, although in the home they seldom find conditions right for growth to more than a metre.

## Climbers and trailers

There are a number of tough, woody-stemmed climbing plants eminently suited to the home. Most durable of all is *Rhoicissus rhomboidea*, the Grape Ivy, which with its glossy dark-green leaves and clinging tendrils can withstand the most severe conditions. Not only is it tolerant of gas fumes and central heating, but it will even survive outdoors over a mild winter, if planted in a very sheltered position. Plants like rhoicissus, and the equally tough ivies, developed from native European plants, are ideal for the home. Some introductions which at first proved very popular are less easy to grow, like *Cissus antarctica*, a plant which looks rather like rhoicissus, but has an annoying tendency to shed its leaves when household fires are lit in the autumn, or when central heating is switched on.

Herbaceous or soft-stemmed climbing and trailing plants grow very rapidly, and are ideal for training against a wall or room divider. Some cling to the wall or to a framework which you can provide, like the many types of philodendron, as well as *Scindapsus aureus*, *Monstera deliciosa*, and *Ficus pumila*.

Tradescantias and their many close relatives trail gracefully and are best grown on shelves, or from hanging baskets, where their soft variegated foliage can be seen to its best advantage. Tradescantias and similar trailing plants are among the easiest to propagate in the home, so a constant supply of fresh new plants can be easily obtained.

## Bromeliads

The natural habitat of bromeliads is usually severe with little or no soil for their roots to grip. They generally live on the branches of jungle trees or on rocky ground, and in the absence of suitable soil nutrients absorb food from a pool of water which accumulates in the centre of their rosette of stiff, spiny leaves. Bromeliads are often attractively coloured and curiously shaped, and their unusual method of feeding means that they are easily cared for in the home.

**The Chinese developed the art of bonsai—the growing of wild trees and shrubs, under certain conditions which result in stunted and distorted replicas of the original plant. It is a difficult and painstaking process but can be accomplished by growing plants in shallow, impoverished soil, pruning the roots to prevent vigorous growth, and physically bending the stems to produce the desired shape.**

## NATURAL PROPAGATION

**1.** In many plants, like sansevieria, shoots are produced from below ground level. In time, these result in the growth of a clump of interconnected plants. The original plant may die off and eventually the clump can cover a considerable area. Typical examples are:
sansevieria
dracaena
pandanus
bromeliads
aglaonema
maranta
calathea
cyperus
aspidistra

**2.** Trailing and climbing plants like the ivies tend to throw out roots wherever their stems touch a suitable growing compost. When these stems become separated from the parent plant, a new plant results. Typical examples are:
trailing philodendrons
syngonium
scindapsus
rhoicissus
cissus
gynura
*Senecio macroglossus*
tradescantia
zebrina
setcreasea
helxine
*Ficus pumila*
*Hoya carnosa*
*Monstera deliciosa*

**3.** Many plants grow from underground storage organs, which spread and branch through the soil. These may be either rhizomes, which are creeping stems, or tubers, which are swollen roots. Each of the branching tips develops its own shoot, which eventually forms a new plant. Typical examples are:
tuberous begonias
caladium
acorus
achimenes
ferns

**4.** A few plants produce runners; thin shoots which travel out across the soil surface, and produce young plants at their tips. Typical examples are:
chlorophytum
*Saxifraga sarmentosa*

**5.** Like rhizomes and tubers, bulbs are storage

organs, being swollen underground buds. Small bulbils divide off from the parent plant, and each will ultimately develop into a new plant. Typical examples are:
tulip
narcissus
lilium
hippeastrum
freesia
hyacinth

**6.** Corms also resemble bulbs, and are swollen and shortened stems. Daughter corms are produced from the previous year's corm, resulting in a clump of new plants. Typical examples are:
crocus
gladiolus
anemone
cyclamen

**7 and 8.** Hundreds of species of cacti and succulents are available, and these share the curious habit of shedding leaves or parts of stems, which promptly take root. Typical examples are:
opuntia
mammillaria
chamaecereus
echinocactus
echeveria
epiphyllum
zygocactus
kleinia
crassula
sedum
euphorbia

**9.** A few unusual plants produce 'baby' plants on their leaves or shoots. These drop off fully formed, and quickly take root. Typical examples are:

*Tolmiea menziesii*
*Asplenium bulbiferum*
*Bryophyllum tubiflorum*
(also known as *Kalanchoe tubiflora*)
*Bryophyllum daigremontianum*

**10.** Many ferns propagate by means of creeping underground rhizomes, like the common bracken. They also produce microscopic spores which are spread by the wind, and consequently can take root at a considerable distance from the parent plant. Typical examples are:
adiantum
pteris
asplenium
platycerium (an epiphyte)
nephrolepis

# New developments

Recent years have seen the perfecting of two growing techniques for indoor plants which had previously been tried for many years—with mixed success. These are hydroponics, the growing of plants in a soil-less medium with a nutrient bathing the roots, and artificial-light gardening, which frees the plant from seasonal variations in natural light intensity. Besides these, the development of foliar feeding has been another important advance for growing plants successfully in the home.

## Hydroponics

Hydroponics is a promising concept the possibilities of which have been considered for many years. Once botanists and agriculturists had worked out the basic nutrients which plants need for healthy growth, there seemed to be no reason why, in theory at least, plants could not be grown with their roots dipped into a solution of nutrients. This would mean that the grower had absolute control over the rate of growth, and soil-borne pests and diseases would be eliminated.

In practice, hydroponics seldom worked reliably. If too much nutrient was available the plant died. It proved very difficult to keep the water conditions stable enough for healthy growth. The new technique seems to overcome all the problems. Developed by Rochfords, the giant British horticulturists, the technique they call 'hydroculture' makes use of two innovations. One is an inert growing medium called hydroleca, which is composed of pellets of clay fired into porous granules about one centimetre in diameter. These absorb water and nutrients, and form a support for the plants' roots.

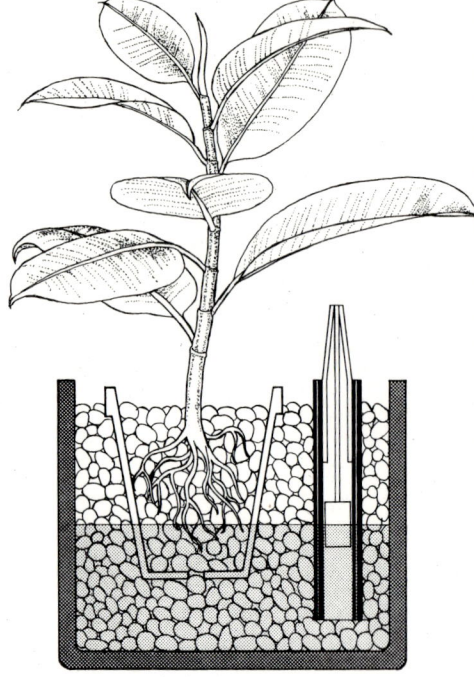

▲ The technique of hydroculture allows plants to be grown in an almost disease-free environment. A gauge indicates when water has to be added and a special feed is given once a year.

The other ingredient is a special fertilizer, which is combined with an ion-exchange resin, in the form of sugar-like granules. This resin resembles the material used in water-softeners, and liberates the fertilizer very slowly and steadily over a period of six to twelve months, maintaining the correct balance of chemicals at all times.

Hydroleca and resin are placed in a special container having a water-level indicator with a pointer, or a sight-glass like a garage petrol pump. All that is required is to add ordinary tap water to keep the water in the container at the specified level.

Because of the ready availability of nutrients, plants grown by hydroculture have quite small root systems, and can live healthily in a container which would normally be much too restricted. Some plants normally classed as 'delicate' seem easier to grow using the hydroculture system, probably partly because of the benefits already mentioned, and also because of the high degree of humidity around the container, due to water evaporating from the hydroleca granules.

## Light gardens

The perfecting of artificial-light gardening means that plants no longer have to be carefully sited in the room to obtain the optimum amount of light. Ordinary light bulbs will provide sufficient light for hardier plants to grow, but have a number of disadvantages. Sunlight carries a mixture of all the colours seen in the rainbow. In most types of artificial light, the proportions of these constituent colours vary so much from sunlight that the growth of the plant is distorted. Light bulbs also have the severe disadvantage of producing so much heat that they soon scorch delicate foliage. The ordinary fluorescent light tube produces light even more unsuitable in colour balance than that produced by light bulbs, but there are several types which produce the kind of light needed for healthy growth. The 'Gro-lux' tube produces a mauvish-coloured light which actually accentuates the natural colours of the plants' leaves and flowers. There is also the 'True-lite' tube which simulates natural daylight.

Gro-lux tubes can be fitted into commercial fluorescent fittings over a plant trough, or on the underside of a shelf suspended over the plant. Most plants thrive with about 20 watts of light for each square 30 cm of growing area, and with the tubes suspended about 30 cm above the plants, although some experimentation will be necessary to find the ideal combination. If plants seem too leggy, they are simply raised nearer the tube, where the light is stronger.

One very important point in artificial-light gardening is that *all metal parts and light fittings must be earthed*. There is a very high humidity above plant troughs, and condensation will form on the fittings, making short circuits a distinct possibility. Holes must be drilled to allow air to circulate through the light fittings, and permit condensation to drain from the diffusers over the tubes. It is best to have a professional electrician wire up your equipment if you try artificial-light gardening. The expense of the whole exercise is well worth

▼ A rooting bag, consisting of sterilized compost into which cuttings are inserted, is a modern aid in propagating plants.

while in that you will be able to raise beautiful plants throughout the year.

## Foliar feeding

The basic nutrients the plant needs are obtained from the thin film of water surrounding soil particles. These are nitrogen, potash and phosphorous, which are generally present in adequate amounts in the compost, and are replaced when repotting or potting-on. Small quantities of other elements are just as important, and these are quite likely to be deficient. For example, a shortage of iron or magnesium may cause yellowing of the leaves. Less common substances like boron and molybdenum are just as important, although the plant uses them only in minute quantities.

Foliar feeding is a new development which puts all these essential chemicals into the plant in a novel way—through the leaves. Certain forms of these nutrients are able to be absorbed through the leaves extremely rapidly, and find their way through the entire plant system by normal water conduction. This process, therefore, is the reverse of the usual method whereby nutrients are brought up from the roots.

With these foliar feeds, which are sprayed on in a very dilute form, there is little or no wastage of fertilizer—it all goes straight into the plant. Additional additives are included, such as the plant growth stimulants niacinamide and vitamin H. These are not normally needed by the plant, but their presence causes marked acceleration of growth and they are well worthwhile when growing plants under the unnatural conditions of the home.

The plant cuticle, or waxy layer on the upper leaf surface, is intended to make the leaf shed water, so it is advisable to spray foliar feeds on the underside of the leaves, using a fine mist sprayer which will not produce large water droplets. A wetting

## DEVELOPMENT OF THE POINSETTIA

**Wild Mexican plant**

**1825 Introduction into the United States by Joel Poinsett**

The poinsettia, *Euphorbia pulcherrima*, is an excellent example of selective breeding. The original plant, growing wild in Mexico, is a large shrub, with coarse leaves and a smallish flower. It was introduced into the United States in 1825 by the US Ambassador to Mexico, Joel Poinsett, and was widely cultivated in botanical gardens and parks. Early this century, Albert Ecke began commercial development of the poinsettia, which at that time was so tall that it could only be sold as a cut flower. By 1929, his son had developed a shorter-growing poinsettia, with larger bracts or false 'petals', called 'Mrs Paul Ecke'. One of the most common modern varieties is the brilliant red 'Barbara Ecke Supreme'.

**1833**
John Bartram and Robert Buist cultivate plant

**1909**
The Ecke family

**1923**
Mr Enteman

True Red

Early Red

Oak Leaf

**1924**
Louis Bordet

Red Sport

Mrs Paul Ecke

St Louis

Ruth Ecke

Barbara Ecke Supreme

Ecke Pink

Ecke White

Indianapolis Red

**1960s**
Norway

Annette Hegg

White Hegg

Pink Hegg

Marbled Hegg

Dark Red Hegg

In the 1960s another major strain was developed in Norway, by the Hegg family, which resulted in a series of entirely new varieties with multi-flowered heads, many having marbled flowers. These culminated in the dwarf poinsettias now so common in florists' displays.

agent is usually incorporated to help the foliar feed adhere to the leaves for long enough to be absorbed.

Do not be tempted to use ordinary liquid fertilizers as a foliar feed. Not only will they fail to be absorbed, but they will scorch the leaves and produce unsightly deposits as they dry.

## Think 'plant'

In spite of all the advances made in the past few years in keeping exotic plants in the home, there are some people who seem to have a 'Brown Thumb'. Even the most hardy plants enter into a slow decline as soon as they are brought into their homes, and no amount of good advice or extra care makes any improvement in their condition. On the other hand, there are those of us who purchase the most exotic and delicate plants, ignore all the instructions on the growers' label, and watch them flourish

▲ Some people believe plants respond to music and the emotions and feelings of their owners. A new explanation for 'green fingers'?

mightily. Can it be that plants are sensitive to their owners' personalities?

There is indeed some scientific evidence to support this view, although needless to say, not all scientists take it too seriously. In February 1966 an American called Cleve Backster, an ex-CIA man now running a school for lie-detector operators, decided to try hooking up a *Philodendron scandens* to one of his lie-detector machines. When he applied a lighted match to one of the leaves, nothing much happened, but when he *considered* burning the leaf for the second time, the polygraph recorded a violent response, from which he concluded that the plant had read his mind.

His next experiment was to find if the plant would respond to another plant's distress. He arranged for a colleague to 'murder' a plant by uprooting it and pulling it to pieces, in the presence of his wired-up specimen. Thereafter, when the 'murderer' came into the room, the wired-up plant responded violently, literally swooning with fear.

Backster also found that his plants responded to the death of shrimps dropped into boiling water, and even to the 'death' of fertilized chicken eggs. This remarkable sensitivity of plants to other forms of life caused something of a stir in the scientific world. Other researchers claimed they had got similar results and one is said to be able to use the leaves of his plants as electrical switches sensitive to his thoughts, with which he can control a toy train.

All this leads to the obvious conclusion that if your plants are not thriving, perhaps they just don't like you. More practically, it has been suggested that plants which unaccountably die off may have been subjected to negative thoughts from their owners. Perhaps the solution is to try to think 'plant', and to try and empathise with your potted captives, making positive efforts to keep them happy.

# Environment

## Water

Although water is the staff of life for a plant, most people tend to overdo the watering, and kill the plant with kindness. The plant's need for water varies enormously at different times of the year. In the spring, and during the summer, when a healthy plant is growing at its fastest, the need for water is at its greatest. Plants which have obviously water-filled tissues, like impatiens and coleus, have a very heavy demand for water, and wilt rapidly if kept too dry. Slow-growing plants like aglaonema, the larger species of ficus, and sansevieria do not use water so rapidly, however, although they still need to be kept moist. Water, even though taken straight from the tap, contains vital chemicals needed for healthy plant growth.

## Warmth

Although many of the plants decorating our homes are tropical in origin, very few will thrive in a temperature over 24°C. A comfortable room temperature of 18 to 21°C suits most indoor plants, although some will live at a lower temperature.

A few indoor plants actually dislike high temperatures, especially in winter when their growth is halted and the plant becomes dormant. The ivies, aspidistra, *Cissus antarctica*, fatshedera, fatsia, azaleas, and a number of other quite hardy plants will

◀ The conservatory or garden room is often built on to the back of a house, forming part of the living accommodation. Being well-lit and warmed by heat radiating from the rest of the house, it is an ideal plant environment. Plants which grow too large for the rest of the house can usually develop to attractive display specimens. In colder weather, a paraffin convector stove is a useful form of heating. In addition to being cheap in operation, it has the advantage of producing large amounts of water vapour which raises the humidity of the room.

# CONDITIONS IN YOUR HOME

The conditions in your home will vary enormously from room to room, even if it is centrally heated or well insulated. For this reason it is difficult to recommend any particular plant as being suitable for a specific room. Generally speaking, however, kitchens tend to be continually warm and humid, and are the most suitable place for delicate moisture-loving plants. Bathrooms are also humid, but only when in use, and for the rest of the time they may be cold and poorly lit. In these conditions, a tender plant will be liable to fungal diseases, and will certainly not thrive. Similarly, before you purchase a plant to stand in a hallway, give some thought to the environment it provides. Most hallways are unheated in the winter, subject to cold draughts when the front door is opened, and poorly lit. On the other hand, they are usually fairly spacious, and so are suitable for large hardy plants like palms, fatshedera, ivies and a number of others. Small porches can get very hot, especially if they face south, and may get quite cold at night. If the light is strong enough, this may mean that the porch is suitable for growing cacti, which naturally experience these conditions. Experiment with your plants if they do not seem to thrive. Try moving them to different positions, where they may be out of a draught of which you were not aware. Water in the atmosphere is more

Morning sun

Wandering Jew

Urn Plant

Sweethe
Plant

Aspidistra

Asparagus

Swiss Chee
Plant

Devil's

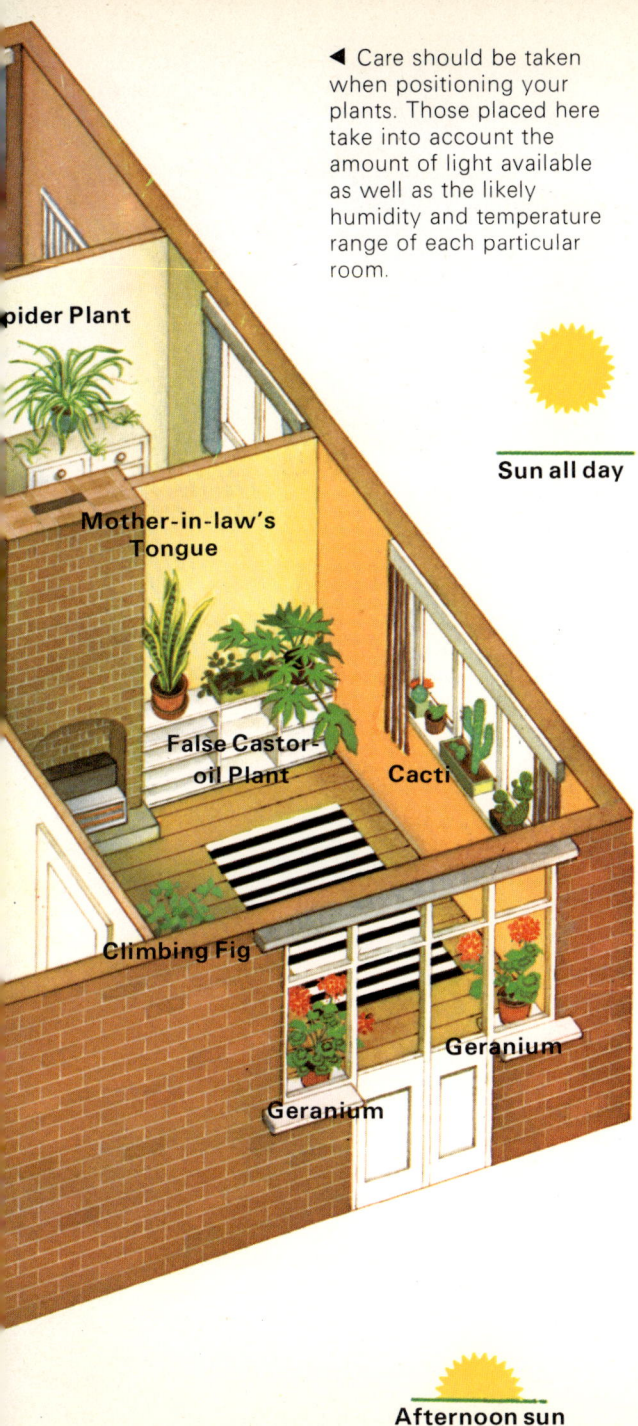

◀ Care should be taken when positioning your plants. Those placed here take into account the amount of light available as well as the likely humidity and temperature range of each particular room.

**Spider Plant**

**Mother-in-law's Tongue**

**Sun all day**

**False Castor-oil Plant**

**Cacti**

**Climbing Fig**

**Geranium**

**Geranium**

**Afternoon sun**

critical, and much more difficult to control. The atmosphere in a centrally heated house is very low in humidity, so that water often evaporates faster from the leaves than it can be replaced by water passing up the stem from the roots. When this happens, the plant wilts and may die or become scorched. Ducted warm-air central heating is particularly bad in this respect, and the continuous warm draught will scorch most types of indoor plants. You can get around the problem by the expensive expedient of providing a humidifier unit to put moisture back into the atmosphere of the room, but it is easier to alter the local conditions of the plant—the microclimate. Plants grown in fern cases, the modern terrarium or bottle gardens, thrive because of the constant high humidity. Even without this protection, you can increase the local humidity around the plant by plunging the pot in a tub or large container full of moist peat or gravel. Water evaporates from this container continuously, and increases the humidity around the plant. If this fails, the only way to preserve the plants is to try keeping them in a room which has a damper atmosphere, like the kitchen or bathroom, although a daily spraying with water may save the situation.

happily withstand winter temperatures only a few degrees above freezing, and do not appreciate high room temperatures at all until their new growth begins in the spring.

Most of the common hardy indoor plants will withstand a winter temperature of not less than 7°C, although probably 15°C is a sensible minimum temperature to aim for.

At very high temperatures the growth rate of plants is accelerated, and they need bright light and adequate water to keep up with this growth. Plants raised in heated greenhouses are growing at this rapid rate, and need 'hardening-off' in slightly cooler conditions before they are ready for cultivation in the home. This is a point to look out for if you buy plants direct from the nursery; make sure they are not taken straight from an overheated greenhouse, if they are, make sure the plants are kept out of draughts for a few weeks.

## Air

During the night, plants absorb oxygen from the air and release carbon dioxide, reversing this process during the daylight, when photosynthesis starts. This constant cycle means that plants can thrive in a sealed bottle garden, where they constantly recycle their own waste products.

It also means that during this cycle they take in undesirable pollutants in the air, which may ultimately poison them. Gas fumes often cause problems in certain sensitive plants. Open coal fires and paraffin convectors can also damage plants. Generally speaking, plants with thick leathery leaves, like *Ficus elastica*, the peperomias, and palms can withstand atmospheric pollutants best, although hair lacquers and aerosol cleaning sprays can overcome even the most durable plants.

What plants need is fresh air, just as much as we do ourselves. This does not

mean draughts, which scorch leaves and, in the winter, can cause frost damage on plants near windows. A gentle breeze on a mild summer day, through a wide-open window, can only improve the health of your plants. But a draught whistling under an ill-fitting door, during the winter while the plant is dormant, can often kill off or weaken a plant so that rots set in, particularly if the soil in the pot has become cold and waterlogged.

## Light

Without light, photosynthesis cannot take place and a plant will die. A plant grown in correct lighting is compact and bushy, with vivid green foliage. If it is a variegated form, the colouring will be intense. But if the light is insufficient the plant will try to bring its leaves closer to the light source, in an attempt to rectify the situation. It becomes tall and leggy, and the green chlorophyll in its leaves breaks down, turning the leaves yellow and blotchy. In a variegated plant, the attractive coloration disappears in a poor light to be replaced by plain green,

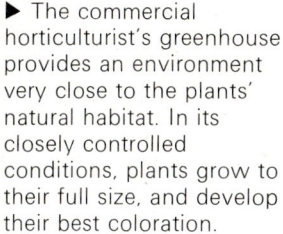

◀ In offices and banks, a display of indoor plants adds beauty to the decor. Many plants thrive in the constant environment provided by the air-conditioning in these buildings.

▶ The commercial horticulturist's greenhouse provides an environment very close to the plants' natural habitat. In its closely controlled conditions, plants grow to their full size, and develop their best coloration.

as the plant manufactures extra chlorophyll in an attempt to use all the available light for photosynthesis.

New shoots grow directly towards the light, making it necessary to rotate the pots occasionally to straighten the growth.

The length of daylight, and the actual type of light falling on the plant are also important. Flowering is triggered off by an inbuilt mechanism which senses the length of the hours of daylight. Zygocactus, the Christmas Cactus, flowers during the shortest days of the year, as does *Euphorbia pulcherrima*, the poinsettia. Other plants, like cacti, need prolonged sunlight before they will flower.

Cacti and succulents also need direct sunlight if they are to thrive, so they are ideal for growing on south-facing window ledges, where very high temperatures may be reached in the direct sunlight. Most other plants grow in lightly shaded conditions beneath trees, so they should be grown indoors out of direct sunlight, which would scorch the foliage. None will survive deeply shaded conditions, but indoors, white-painted ceilings and walls often reflect sufficient light for adequate growth. Artificial light gardening, although expensive to set up, frees your plants from the limitation of natural light and the season, and allows you to vary the flowering and growing cycles of your plants at will.

## Cleanliness

Carbon dioxide, oxygen, and water vapour pass in and out of the foliage of your plants through microscopic pores called stomata. These are easily clogged by dust and grime, so air-borne dirt, as well as looking unsightly, can ruin the health of your plants. It also contains atmospheric pollutant chemicals which can damage the foliage. Regular cleaning with a damp cloth removes this dirt safely. Some people use commercial foliage treatments containing specially developed waxes which give the leaves a brilliant sheen. These should not be used on the underside of the leaves, however, as the wax could clog the stomata. For the same reason, household waxes, oils, and milk should not be used on the leaves. It is far better to use lukewarm water.

# Buying a plant

Choosing an indoor plant is a matter of commonsense. You don't need to be an expert to know that a plant with wilting foliage is not in good condition. If the compost in its pot is too wet, or dried out, it is probable that the plant has been neglected for some time, so it should be avoided.

A healthy plant has glossy, evenly coloured leaves, and plenty of buds on its growing shoots. Look out for scorch-marks on the leaves, or for patchy coloration which could indicate virus disease. If you are buying a flowering plant, it is usually advisable to look for one where the flowers are just on the point of opening. In azaleas, for example, you will usually find one or two flowers open, to give you an indication of their colour, while the rest of the plant contains a mass of developing buds.

When buying any plant your best guide is knowledge. You should know in advance roughly what you are looking for, and be guided by the labels on the pots. Some major horticulturists grade their plants to give an idea of how easy they are to cultivate. Those marked 'Intermediate' or 'Easy' are worth trying in most homes, but those with a 'Delicate' label require specialized treatment, and you would have to consider if you could provide suitable conditions for them or otherwise resign yourself to the probability of seeing them deteriorate after a few weeks.

## Exotic but frail

Unfortunately, it is a general rule that the more exotic-looking a plant is, the more difficult it is to care for it. This applies especially with variegated and brightly coloured plants like *Begonia rex*, codiaeum, dracaena, caladium, cordyline, and maranta. It is always best to try a plant with plain foliage first. If you find it grows successfully in your home, by all means try one of its variegated relations, which should thrive, though they will grow less rapidly.

This rule does not always apply with flowering indoor plants, where it is well worth looking out for plants where the name on the label is followed by the description 'F₁ hybrid'. This means that the plant is a hybrid grown from two dissimilar parents. It will show 'hybrid vigour', and be larger and more spectacular than either of its parents. Don't bother to try and grow further plants from the seed your plant produces as they would not breed true.

◄ Buying a plant on impulse can prove embarrassing, particularly if it is just not suitable for your home.

▲ Although all plants need adequate light for healthy growth, only a few will tolerate direct sunlight.

▲ Buying a healthy plant is a matter of commonsense. A healthy looking, well-coloured plant probably *is* healthy.

► Horticultural oddities, like the Venus Fly Trap, rarely grow into the splendid plant depicted on the labels.

## Play safe

Some garden centres and even supermarkets stock novelties; unusual and exotic plants which are usually supplied in a dormant condition in gaily illustrated containers. The Venus Fly Trap, an interesting carnivorous plant, is often supplied in this way. Other exotic plants of this type are Banana plants, Breadfruit, and some of the larger palms. Try them out by all means, but don't expect them to produce plants like those shown on the pack. Such novelties are almost without exception temperamental and difficult for the non-specialist to grow. If you insist on buying oddities, stick to cacti and succulents, which are undemanding, and come in a range of shapes, colours, and sizes to suit the most inquisitive indoor gardener.

## Plant maintenance

When you get your new acquisition home, don't be in too much of a hurry to add fertilizer to the pot—it probably already has enough, and will need a while to acclimatize itself to its new home before it needs feeding. Even though its pot might look too small, remember that the plant has been growing in it quite happily, so just knock it out and check that there is enough room for the roots before deciding to repot.

# Materials and equipment

Care of indoor plants can be made as straight-forward, or as complicated, as you wish. You can keep things very simple by just repotting plants occasionally, but to get the best from them you will need a few simple gadgets and some basic materials, many of which you will be able to improvise.

A vast range of plant holders can be purchased varying from simple decorative sleeves for plant pots, to expensive china pots. Some of the tools and materials used on your garden will come in useful, but if this is your first venture in cultivating plants, you can still succeed with a minimum of outlay.

Your most basic tool for indoor gardening is a watering can. This does not mean the 7-litre capacity can used in garden or greenhouse, but one specially designed for the job, with a long, narrow spout. Don't try and make do with a jug, for the flow of water will wash soil away from the roots of your plants, and if the foliage spreads over the side of the pot you will not be able to hold the jug close enough to avoid slopping water.

Scarcely less important is a sprayer. Small inexpensive plastic spray guns are available which deliver a very fine mist of water. They are also very useful for applying pesticides and foliar feeds (fertilizers applied to the leaves).

The normal garden trowel and fork are rather large for work with indoor plants, and miniature versions can be purchased at garden centres. However, you can very easily improvise by using an ordinary table fork and spoon when repotting or planting small indoor plants. The dibber is another simple gadget to make, consisting simply of a tapered and pointed stick which is used to punch holes in the compost, into which small plants can be dropped and firmed in.

When you are ready to try propagating your plants from cuttings or seed, a propagator is a worthwhile investment. Some are large and expensive devices capable of holding several plant trays, and even having their own heating system, like a small greenhouse. A simple unheated propagator capable of holding about six pots is usually quite big enough for the amateur indoor gardener, but make sure that you buy one which has adjustable ventilators, to avoid excess condensation. Some very small types are available, which will hold a single pot and stand comfortably on a windowsill.

### Gardening materials
A variety of general gardening materials come in useful. If you grow climbing or twining plants, you will probably need to extend the sticks or the trellis supplied with the young plants. Thin bamboo canes can be tied with plastic-covered garden wire into trellises and frames of the appropriate size. You can make most attractive climbing frames by bending

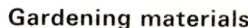

split canes into decorative shapes before wiring them together. This can be done by holding them over a lighted gas ring, bending them, and holding the bend in place until the bamboo has cooled.

Plants with aerial roots and ivies, thrive best if these roots are allowed to grow into damp sphagnum moss, which you can bind around a cane. Using heavy plastic netting, you can also make a decorative column packed with moss and peat, up which your plants will climb.

Another important group of accessories are chemicals; the fertilizers, pesticides, and other materials which help keep plants in the peak of health. You will not need too many pesticides, as indoor plants are relatively isolated from disease and pests, unlike those grown in the garden. Fertilizers are especially valuable indoors, as a rapidly growing plant very soon exhausts the limited food supply in a pot, and you would otherwise be constantly repotting.

### Moisture meters
Some specialized gadgets for the indoor gardener are moisture meters, which are plunged into the compost rather like cooking thermometers, and quickly tell you if the soil is becoming stale and waterlogged. Hygrometers measure the amount of moisture in the atmosphere of the room. A reading of 50 to 75 is considered normal, although some plants like it damper still. Readings near 100 are obtained in uncomfortably damp rooms, but in the winter, in a centrally heated house, they may drop to about 15; conditions few plants will withstand for long.

### Compost
All plants need some form of compost in which to grow, but resist the temptation to use garden soil, however fertile it may look. Composts prepared for indoor plants are carefully designed to have precisely the required texture and constituents. Even more important, they are free of pests, diseases, and possible pollutants which may not harm the tough plants living naturally in our climate, but could have a disastrous effect on the more delicate indoor plants.

Several standard types of potting compost for indoor plants are available, many under proprietary names. Some are specifically intended for certain types of plants, like mixtures for acid-loving or lime-hating plants; azaleas, heathers, camellias, begonias, saintpaulias, and cyclamen.

John Innes mixtures are soil-based composts which have been found, by long experience, to be very suitable for a wide range of plants. They are available in a range of formulations known as JI 1, JI 2 and JI 3.

More recently a range of soilless or peat-based composts have been developed, which are much cleaner to handle and do not need sterilizing or complex mixing. They are based on a general mixture of equal volumes of peat and sand, with added fertilizer, and are probably best purchased ready mixed. They are usually supplied in a single grade, unlike the John Innes composts, and contain sufficient nutrients to last for several months before additional fertilizer is necessary. If you use peat-based composts, you must be very sure that your plants are watered correctly, as once the compost has dried out thoroughly water tends to flow straight through the pot without soaking in.

### Potting materials
1 Peat
2 Hydroleca
3 Hoof and horn
4 Potting compost
5 Silver sand
6 Bone-meal
7 Potting compost
8 Charcoal
9 Cactus medium

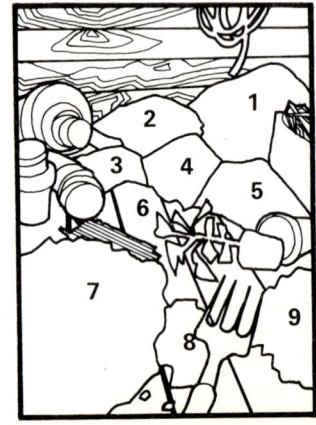

# Watering and feeding

Next to light, water is the most essential requirement for a plant. It is also capable of killing a plant if applied too heavily, or at the wrong time of year. It is important to understand the plant's water requirements. These will be heavy at times of maximum growth in spring and summer, or in flowering plants when the buds are about to open. In the winter, growth stops almost entirely, and pots can be allowed to dry out, watering lightly only once or twice each month, and resuming normal watering when signs of new growth are seen in the spring.

The majority of house plants can be watered simply by filling the gap between the surface of the compost and the rim of the pot, using a narrow-spouted watering can. Don't use icy-cold water, and allow it all to soak through into the soil before adding more. If the water drains through the pot into the saucer, tip the excess away. There are only a

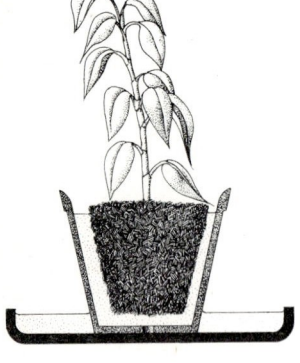

few plants which like to stand in water, such as helxine or Mind-Your-Own Business, and cyperus, a reed-like plant.

If you let the compost dry out too much, it will shrink

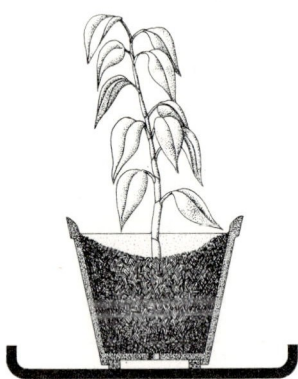

away from the side of the pot into a tight mass. When you water the plant, the water will run straight through the pot, leaving the centre of the root quite dry and hard.

On the other hand, you may find that water lies on the surface of the compost, and hardly soaks in at all. This does not mean that a plant has had enough water, but that the compost has become compacted down so hard that water cannot enter. Compost in this condition cannot long support healthy growth. It is usually a sign that all the soil nutrients are exhausted. If this is not speedily rectified, the roots

will rot and kill the entire plant.

There is a simple remedy for both of these conditions. The surface of the compost

must be pricked over with a small fork or dibber, trying to avoid too much disturbance of the roots. Now stand the pot in a large container, supporting it on a plant saucer or some crocks. Fill the con-

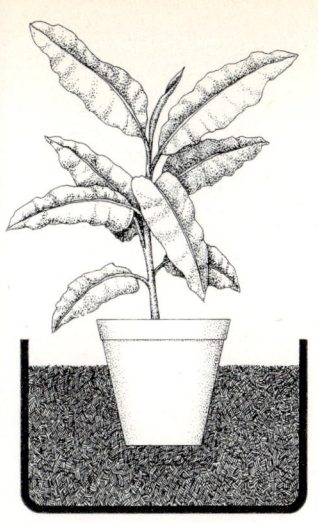

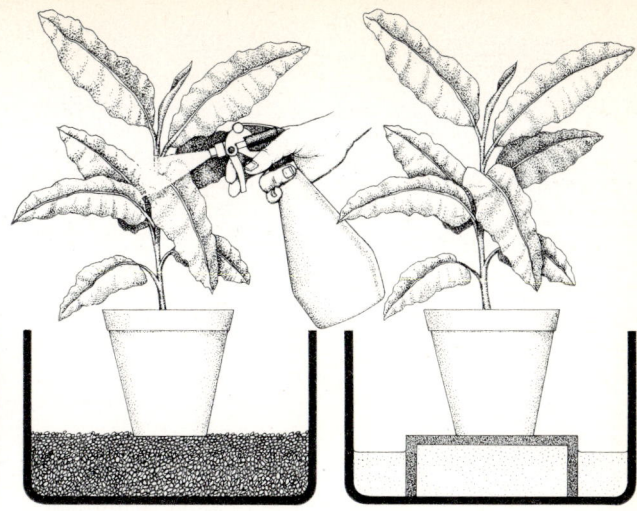

▲ Placing a pot plant in moist peat helps keep the compost moist and humidity around the plant high.

▲ A damp gravel bed increases local humidity and prevents waterlogging. Spraying helps prevent wilting.

▲ Humidity can be increased by standing the pot above water. A few plants may be grown partially submerged.

tainer with lukewarm water until the level is near that of the surface of the compost. Leave it to soak for a couple of hours, then let it drain before replacing the pot in its normal position. You should consider if your plant needs repotting, as these can be warning signs.

This watering technique should be used as a routine with saintpaulias, cyclamen, and sinningia (gloxinia), which dislike having their foliage wetted.

The water you use can come straight from the tap, with a dash of warm water to take off the chill. The only exceptions are lime-hating plants like azaleas, grevilleas, cyclamen and orchids, which are best watered with rainwater which has been allowed to settle in a water

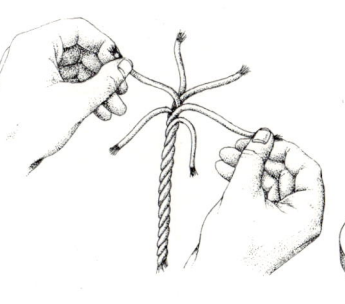

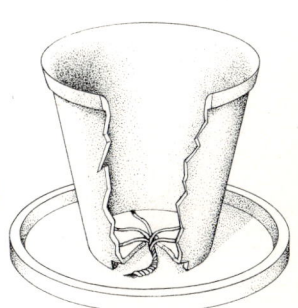

▲ A simple wick improves the water supply to your plants. Obtain a cotton or glass-fibre wick from a hardware store, and fray out the ends.

▲ Knock out the plant and push the wick through the drainage hole. Keep the saucer topped up with water. The pot *must* be supported above the water.

butt for a while, or with soft water obtained from the ice accumulating in a freezer or refrigerator, which can be collected during defrosting.

If your plants stand on a

windowsill, avoid getting water droplets on the foliage; this will cause scorching if the plant is in direct sunlight. In hard-water areas, water droplets leave white lime spots on the leaves, especially obvious in dark-leaved plants like ivies, ficus, and cordyline.

Water is equally important in the atmosphere around your plants. If they do not thrive, or if their leaves wilt or become scorched, the atmosphere is probably too dry. You can increase the humidity locally by several methods.

The most convenient technique is to plunge the pot into a larger container filled with damp peat. Evaporation from the peat keeps the surrounding atmosphere

▼ Plants can suffer while you are on holiday. Small water dispensers can be purchased which allow water to dribble out slowly into the soil. You can improvise a waterer using coarse string as a wick to syphon water from a jam jar into the plant pot.

moist, especially if there are no draughts.

Cyclamen and saintpaulias sometimes benefit from a light steam bath. They should be stood in a large container, supported clear of the bottom. Hot water is added, sufficient to nearly reach the bottom of the pot, bathing the leaves in warm, moist water vapour. After five minutes, remove the plant and replace it in its usual position.

## Fertilizers
Most fertilizers contain three basic nutrients; nitrogen, phosphates, and potassium. Each has a particular function. A plant starved of nitrogen, for example, is stunted and has pale green leaves. Phosphate deficiency causes weak root systems, and potassium deficiency makes plants generally spindly and prone to disease.

Commercial fertilizers contain all these substances,

▼ Add water to the top of a fern cylinder, and to the pot at the base.

and several 'trace elements' which are necessary for health, even though they are present in only minute quantities. You will need to use fertilizers fairly frequently during the growing period. Peat-based composts and John Innes composts contain sufficient nutrients for about two months' healthy growth before they need 'topping up' with fertilizer, or repotting.

▼ Bulbs grown in a traditional hyacinth glass need only water to bring them into flower. Add a few pieces of charcoal to stop the water becoming foul.

There are several techniques for applying fertilizers. Solid fertilizers like bone-meal and superphosphate can be worked into the surface compost taking care not to disturb the roots. Take care also not to use too much, and water thoroughly after each application.

Pelleted fertilizers containing a variety of nutrients can also be purchased. They are simply dropped into a hole made by a dibber, and firmed over. The plant sends out roots which surround the fertilizer pellet and absorb the nutrient.

Easiest of all to apply are liquid fertilizers which are diluted and simply watered on to the soil surfaces. These are usually supplied in a highly concentrated form

and must be used exactly as instructed by the manufacturers. If too strong a mixture is used the plants will suffer. The soluble concentrated powder fertilizers are the most economical however.

Foliar feeds are a recent innovation. These are specially formulated with nutrients which can be absorbed through the plants' leaves. They are best applied with a fine-mist sprayer, and because they are almost immediately absorbed they can have a remarkable effect on an ailing plant. Some contain vitamins which seem to have a growth-promoting effect.

◄ If you have a bromeliad 'tree', with plants wired to the branches, these will need watering in the centre of their rosettes.

# Growing and potting

If conditions in your home are satisfactory, most plants will grow well, and soon need some routine attention. Many will outgrow their pots, and need repotting or potting-on; these techniques are described below. Just as important is the care of the parts of your plants which are on show— the stems, flowers, and foliage. Cut off flowers as soon as they are past their best, and the plant will usually produce more. Dead or withered leaves must be snipped off—they may be diseased—and don't be afraid to cut off other parts of the plant which look straggly; it will encourage bushy and healthy growth.

Your plant pot or container is important in maintaining the health of your plant. When you purchase a plant, it is probably growing in a reasonably sized pot, but it

### ▼ Types and sizes of pots
**1** Orchid pot
**2** Half pot
**3** Seed pot
**4** Herb pot
**5** 6.5-cm (2½-in) pot
**6** 9-cm (3½-in) pot
**7** 12.5-cm (5-in) pot
**8** 17.5-cm (7-in) pot
More detailed information on types of pot is given on p. 63.

will soon need potting-on as it grows. Sometimes a plant fails to thrive in spite of regular applications of fertilizer, and in this case, it may need repotting; a slightly different technique. Don't be in too much haste to change plant pots. The plant has grown quite happily in the pot in which it was supplied.

Some people prefer to grow plants in plastic pots, which are clean to handle. Others prefer the traditional clay variety, which are absorbent, and allow water to evaporate so as to maintain a humid atmosphere about the plant, and air to circulate

about the roots. If you do use clay pots which have previously held plants, scald them with boiling water to prevent the introduction of disease, and in any event soak them in water overnight before use.

Many types of pot are available, and among the most useful are those made from foam polystyrene. These are light in weight and rather fragile, but they insulate the plant roots very well, and are ideal for propagating.

Your plants will grow quite happily in a pot that may seem too small. In fact,

the size of the plant bears little relationship to the extent of the root system, and when plants are grown in a rich compost and well supplied with fertilizer they do not need extensive root systems to provide them with adequate nourishment. Periodically you must check to see if the plants' roots are healthy, and if repotting is necessary.

▼ When repotting or potting-on, a layer of peat may be added to retain moisture.

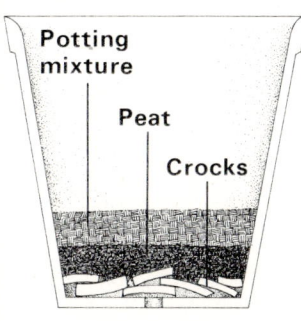

Potting mixture

Peat

Crocks

## Spot the signs

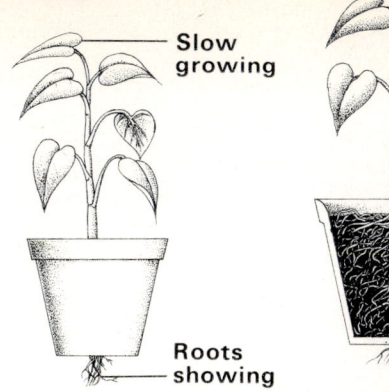

Slow growing

Roots showing

## Pot bound plant

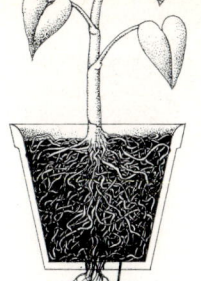

**Plant needs potting-on**

### Inspecting the roots

Place your hand across the top of the pot, so that the stem or stems pass between your fingers. Now turn the pot upside down, and tap the edge of the pot sharply against a table top or a potting bench. The entire plant, together with the compost, should come out without difficulty, so that the condition of the roots can be examined.

If you have had the pot plunged in a tub of peat, it is quite likely that roots will have emerged through the drain hole at the bottom of the pot. These must be care-fully pushed back as the pot is lifted from the soil-ball.

The soil-ball should hold together in a compact mass. You should see many roots spreading across its surface. These are generally white, and even if many are visible, this does not necessarily mean that the plant has outgrown its pot.

If some of the roots are withered and obviously dead, carefully loosen them from the soil-ball, and trim them off with scissors. If you have previously noted that growth had unaccountably stopped, you will probably find that the soil is either dry and crumbling or else packed down very hard, with no visible air spaces. In either case, loosen the soil with your fingers, taking care not to damage healthy

### Knocking out

**Trimming roots**

43

roots, until you are left with a compact ball of soil around the main roots of the plant.

## Repotting

Now you must repot to give the plant a fresh start. Place some crocks from a broken clay pot in the bottom of the

original pot, and cover with fresh compost. Hold the plant by the stem, and run compost into the pot. When it reaches the rim, press the compost down firmly. Rap the pot sharply on a flat surface to bed down all the compost, top it up to near the rim, and water thoroughly before replacing it in its growing position.

## Potting-on

If, when you knock out the plant for examination, you find the soil-ball a mass of healthy roots, it's time for potting-on to a larger size of pot. This is very simple, and does not seriously disturb the roots. Select a larger pot and, as before, cover the drain holes with broken

crocks. Put a layer of compost over this, thick enough to bring the surface of the original soil-ball up to within 1 cm of the rim of the pot. Now run compost around the soil-ball, firming down with the thumbs. Tamp it down well, and water the plant thoroughly. Depending on the size and type of the plant, the pot used for potting-on should allow about 2 cm more space all round for the roots.

Whether repotting or potting-on, *never use a pot without drainage holes*. Lack of drainage means that the roots will become waterlogged and rotten, and the plant will soon die.

If you have a very large specimen plant like *Monstera deliciosa*, or a large ficus, or a tall palm, it may be very difficult to move it without damage, and repotting may not be feasible. In this case, using a small trowel, remove as much compost from the surface of the pot as possible, taking great care when working

around the roots. Replace with fresh compost, and press this down firmly.

After repotting, potting-on, or top-dressing a large specimen plant, do not be in too much of a hurry to feed the plant. However careful you have been, the roots will have suffered some shock and slight damage, and will need a few weeks to grow into the fresh compost. Leave the fertilizers off for at least 6 weeks, keeping the compost damp with plain tap water.

▼ Add top-dressing to large plants.

## Bulb care

Most bulbs also appreciate a potting compost rich in humus. When you buy bulbs in autumn, they may possibly have been pre-treated to make them come into flower unnaturally early. Plant them in bulb fibre, a special mixture of peat, charcoal, and shell grit, with the crown just below the surface of the firmed-down compost. With hyacinths, narcissi and hippeastrums, allow the crowns to protrude above the surface of the compost. If you want early-flowering bulbs, cover the pot with black poly-

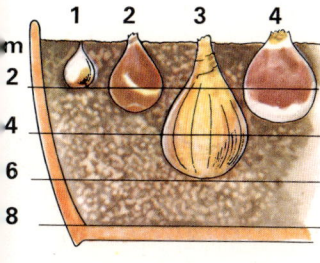

▲ When planting bulbs make sure they do not touch each other nor the sides of the bowl. 1. Small bulbs. 2. Tulips. 3. Daffodils. 4. Hyacinths.

thene, and keep it in a cool place (but one protected from frost). When the shoots are about 4 cm high, remove the polythene and bring the pot into its flowering position, in a light place, but preferably where temperatures are not too high. After flowering, plant the bulbs outdoors, where they may become naturalized.

## Cacti and succulents

Not surprisingly, cacti and succulents demand special treatment. The desert types, like many other indoor plants, require a resting period in a cool room (but protected from frost), with a complete lack of watering from late autumn and through the winter. Start watering again in mid-March, and keep them moist throughout the summer. They will grow quite well in JI 1 compost, although it is best to add additional sand or grit, and if rested as described above many types will flower in profusion. Some types need quite different handling, however; these are the trailing forest cacti, zygocactus, schlumbergera, and epiphyllum. These trailing cacti live naturally on tree branches, like some ferns and orchids, and appreciate a peaty compost, with added sphagnum moss, and a humid atmosphere.

## Ferns

Some plants need special potting techniques. You must be very careful that the compost you use is right for your plants. Be particularly careful when repotting any of the lime-hating plants, as you must use a special compost, usually sold under the name 'ericaceous mixture'.

Give thought to the conditions in which your plant would live in nature. Ferns, for example, generally live in shady positions under trees, so they appreciate composts rich in humus,

such as peat or leaf-mould. You can devise a very attractive fern-column, using heavy-gauge plastic garden netting. This should be rolled up and secured with garden wire, to make a cylinder about 1 m high and 15 cm in diameter. Stuff the cylinder with a mixture of peat-based compost and sphagnum moss, and stand it upright in a plant pot which is also filled with compost. You can now plant a variety of small ferns in the column, into holes made with a dibber, through the open mesh. Water the column by pouring water in at the top, and spray the growing ferns with fresh water periodically.

▼ A fern-column is an effective way of displaying a variety of ferns.

# Propagat-ing

Most indoor plants can be grown from seed, and in the case of flowering plants, especially annuals, this is a quick and inexpensive way to increase your collection. Seed merchants carry stocks of hundreds of annuals and freely-flowering perennials suitable for indoor cultivation. Foliage plants, particularly those with woody stems, are not so easy, but they can usually be grown readily by other methods of propagation.

The propagator is a simple device which maintains a fairly constant humidity and temperature about the young plants. Whether grown from seed, from cuttings, or by some other technique, young developing plants have a feeble root system, and can easily lose water by evaporation more quickly than they can replace it by water drawn from the compost The proper use of a propagator prevents this rapid water loss, and gives the plant an opportunity to develop adequate roots before being faced with the rigours of its normal indoor growing position.

In its simplest form, the propagator can be a clear polythene bag into which the whole pot and plants are placed. Small sticks hold the polythene clear of the plant, and the bag is then twisted shut and secured with an elastic band. Excess condensation must be removed from the inside of the bag by tapping the plastic gently, as otherwise the young plants would rot.

This problem is less likely to occur when using a commercial propagator, which has adjustable ventilators to avoid the build-up of excess condensation. You can fit an entire seed-tray into the propagator, but it is better to grow the plants in individual containers, plunged into damp peat. Plant pots made of compressed peat are particularly useful for this, as the plant and its peat pot can later be transferred direct to a larger pot without disturbing the roots in any way.

Never place the propagator in direct sunlight, or the temperature will rise so high that all your young plants will die. And don't

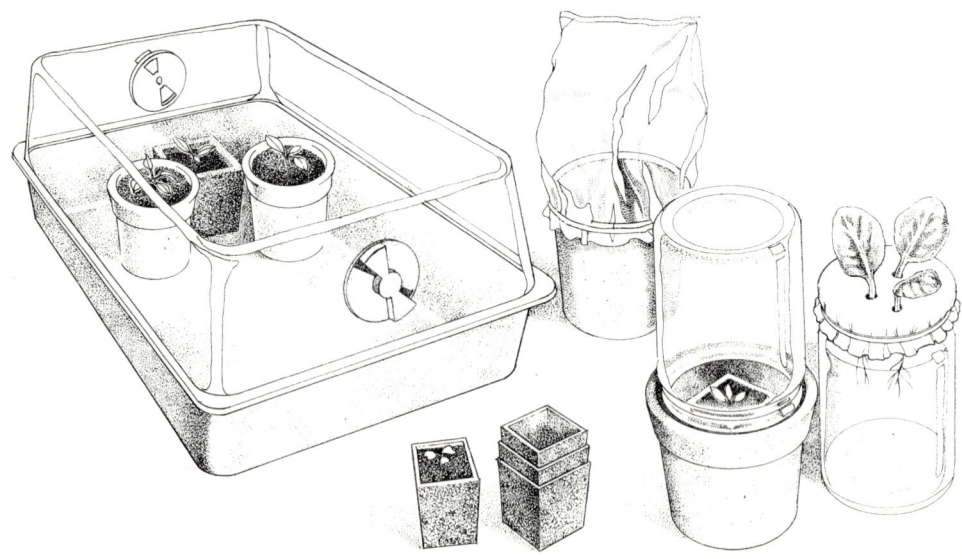

attempt to propagate your plants while they are dormant or not growing rapidly. If cuttings or young plants do not root and develop quickly, they are likely to die off.

Easiest of all to propagate are the types of plants which naturally spread by vegetative means.

## Natural propagation

Chlorophytum, the Spider Plant, sends out long runners which trail over the side of the pot. On these runners a series of plantlets develops. If these runners trail on peat surrounding the pot in a plant trough they quickly take root, and can be severed from the parent plant and potted separately. You can take advantage of this natural process by pegging down the runners on the surface of compost in another pot, or separate them with a sharp knife and plant them out in your propagator.

The Mother-of-Thousands, *Saxifraga sarmentosa*, produces similar rooting runners, as does the Piggy-Back Plant, *Tolmiea menziesii*, and these can be propagated without any difficulty.

Ivies, philodendrons, scindapsus and many other climbing plants with aerial roots are particularly easy to propagate in this manner, as the roots soon become established in any suitable growing medium, allowing the stem to be severed complete with several leaves and the growing shoot.

Plants that form large

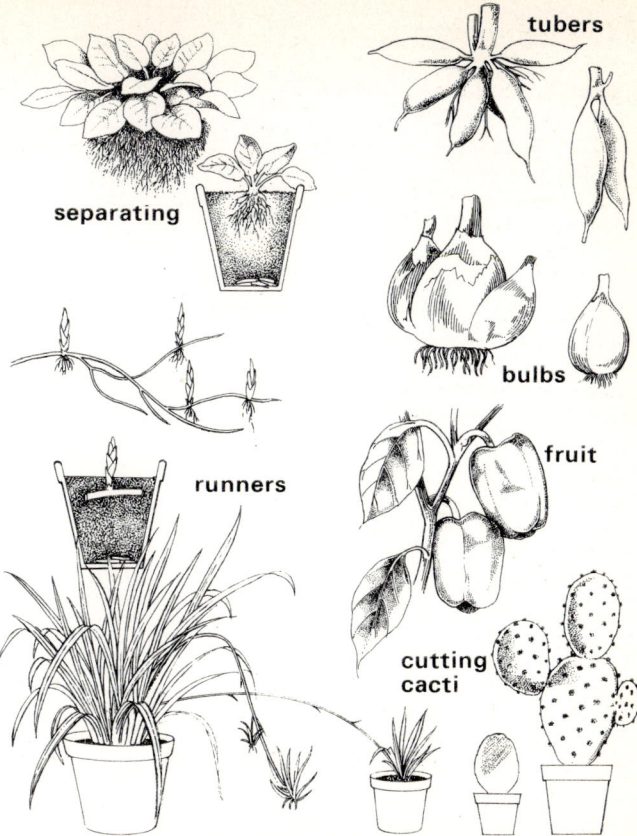

separating

tubers

bulbs

runners

fruit

cutting cacti

clumps, like aspidistra and sansevieria, can be simply knocked out of their pot and pulled gently apart to form a number of separate smaller clumps. Connecting roots or rhizomes must be severed with a sharp knife. In the same way, bulbs and tubers develop small bulblets, and when the soil is gently removed from around the roots during repotting, these can be broken off and planted separately.

Cacti and succulents are also easy to propagate, and because they can tolerate very dry conditions, a

covered propagator is not always necessary. Using a very sandy potting medium, press cut-off or broken segments of cacti into the soil. These segments are best removed by cutting just below the 'joint' on the plant. If they exude much milky sap (latex), blot this off with tissues or by dipping the cuttings into powdered charcoal. Leave them to dry off for a couple of days before planting, laying them on the surface of some clean sand. The leaves of succulents can be rooted using the same method.

## Stem cuttings

'Easy' plants to grow from cuttings, like coleus, tradescantias and their relatives, saintpaulias, impatiens, and fuchsias, will take root quite easily if placed in a jar of water. When the roots have developed to a reasonable size, the cutting can be placed directly into its growing pot, with little need for a propagator.

Cuttings grow best in a moist but very well-drained compost, composed of equal parts of peat and sand. Fertilizer is unnecessary un-

til they have rooted properly.

Another invaluable aid when taking cuttings is the use of rooting powders, which contain plant growth hormones. The base of the cutting is dipped into the hormone powder before being planted, and root growth is considerably stimulated.

For the best results take cuttings deliberately, rather than just nipping off odd sections from your plants. Soft, or non-woody cuttings like those discussed above are the easiest to root. Softwood cuttings from slower-growing plants like pelargoniums (geraniums) and chrysanthemums need a little more care.

Using a sharp knife, take off a length of shoot about 10 cm long, containing at least two leaf nodes (the 'joints' where leaves join the stem). Cut back the stem to just below the lowest node, and remove the last leaf or pair of leaves. If you are using a rooting hormone, dip the base of the cutting in the powder so that it has a good covering. Insert the cutting in moist compost, up to the lowest set of leaves, and place the plant pot in a propagator. Keep the compost moist but not waterlogged, and do not disturb or repot the cutting until it has obviously begun to grow vigorously.

▶ The bryophyllum propagates by discarding the plantlets which grow round the edges of the leaves.

Hardwood cuttings, taken from the woody-stemmed plants, are handled in a similar manner, but they must be larger, and more leaves should be stripped from the lower part of the stem. Make your cutting from the current year's growth, before the stem has become too hard and woody. Rooting hormones are beneficial, and a small amount of sand should be sprinkled into the dibber hole in the compost before planting the cutting. Hardwood cuttings take much longer to become established than do those with soft and fleshy stems.

With any type of cutting blot sap or latex with tissues or powdered charcoal before planting.

▲ Softwood cuttings

▶ Hardwood cutting.

## Leaf cuttings

Like stems, leaves can also be used to make cuttings. For fleshy-leaved plants like saintpaulias, begonias and sinningias (gloxinias) this is the easiest and most effective method of propagation. Saintpaulia leaves can be simply rooted, if suspended over a jar with the stems in the water. They will also root very easily in damp compost. Small plantlets develop from the base of the leaf stem.

Slow-growing long-leaved plants like sansevieria and streptocarpus can be rooted by cutting leaves into short sections and in-serting each piece upright into moist compost. Growth is very slow, and in the case of sansevieria the leaves of the resulting plants will have lost the yellow edging of the parent. This coloration can only be preserved by dividing off shoots produced from the roots of the parent plant.

*Begonia rex, B. masoniana*, and other begonia species with prominent leaf veins can be propagated by cutting up a leaf into triangular or diamond-shaped sections, each about 2 cm long, and with the leaf vein ending at the point of the cutting. These are planted upright in the compost, and must be grown under a propagator. It is advisable to dust begonia leaf cuttings with a fungicide to avoid mildew, to which begonias are especially prone.

A different technique can be used for propagating begonias with prominent leaf veins. Cut across the major veins on the back of the leaf at 2 cm intervals. Place the leaf, with the underside down, on the surface of a pot filled with moist compost, and hold it down with a few small pebbles. Alternatively, use pieces of wire bent into 'U' shapes, and press them through the leaf

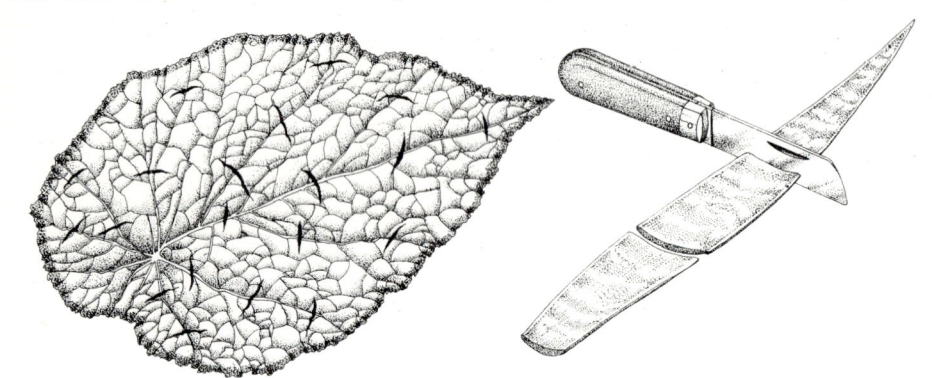

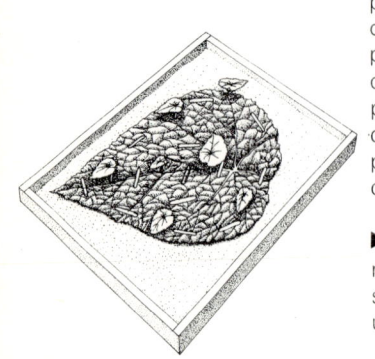

▲ *Begonia rex* may be propagated by leaf-cuttings. A healthy leaf is picked, and the leaf-veins cut through, before being pinned to the surface of damp compost in a propagator. Small plantlets develop from the cuts.

▶ *Sansevieria trifasciata* readily propagates from slivers of leaf placed upright in compost.

and into the compost, securing the leaf-veins tight against the surface. Place the pot in a propagator. Roots will develop at the points where the veins were severed, and soon tiny plants will appear through the slits in the leaf as it withers. Begonia plants produced by leaf-vein cuttings or ordinary leaf cuttings will retain the full coloration of the parent plants. Related plants such as sinningia (gloxinia) and smithiantha (Temple Bells) can also be propagated by leaf-vein cuttings.

## Air layering

Large indoor plants, like *Ficus elastica* and its relatives, *Monstera deliciosa*, fatsia, and fatshedera can be propagated by the different technique of air layering. This is a simple method of propagation which does not damage the parent plant, and is at the same time a good way to improve the appearance of a plant which has grown too tall. A slit is made, about a third of the way through the stem, just below one of the leaf nodes. If the stem is woody, as in *Ficus elastica*, cut out a small ring of bark, taking care not to cut too deeply. Sprinkle rooting hormone liberally over the cut, and if you have slit the stem, press some sphagnum moss into the slit to stop it from closing up. Make up a mixture of $\frac{1}{3}$ peat and $\frac{2}{3}$ sphagnum moss, damp it well, and press it into a compact ball about the cut area, binding this compost with polythene to

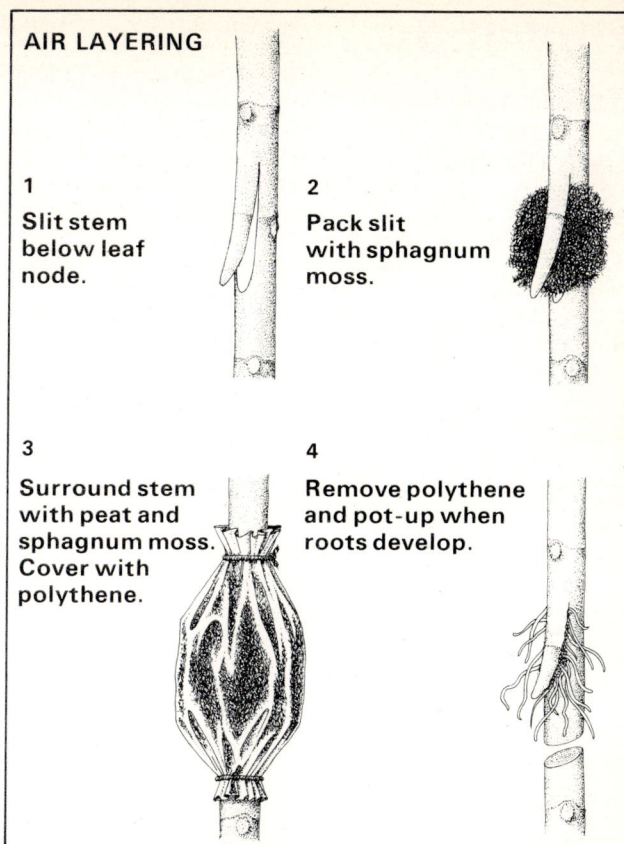

## AIR LAYERING

**1** Slit stem below leaf node.

**2** Pack slit with sphagnum moss.

**3** Surround stem with peat and sphagnum moss. Cover with polythene.

**4** Remove polythene and pot-up when roots develop.

hold it in place. Secure the polythene above and below the cut with elastic bands (not too tight) or with adhesive tape. After a few weeks, roots will develop and can be seen through the polythene. Keep the compost damp until the roots have filled the ball, then cut through the stem just below the newly rooted area, remove the polythene and pot-up your new plant. The remaining section of plant will benefit from having some of its excess growth removed, and should now throw out several side shoots, to make a more bushy plant. Don't try and make your air-layered cutting too large. With ficus species, it is best to make the cut just below the first fully-developed leaf on the plant. In air-layering monstera, your task is made much easier by its tendency to produce long aerial roots, which are normally led back into the pot. Try and make the layering cut near a node bearing aerial roots, and persuade these to grow into the moss and peat mixture, which will speed the development of new roots.

# Pips and herbs

There are many plants which you can grow indoors purely for fun. They will seldom develop into a satisfactory indoor plant, but you will get a good deal of pleasure from keeping them temporarily in your home. These are the plants grown from pips and fruit stones, most of which normally form good-sized trees.

Other plants have a more practical use. You can grow many useful herbs on your kitchen windowsill—right where they will be needed.

Most fruits contain seeds, pips or stones. Provided they have not been cooked, most of these will germinate and grow quite readily indoors, at least until they outgrow their quarters. Oranges and lemons grow very easily in suitable seed compost, producing very attractive dark green foliage. They will not produce fruit, however, except in the greenhouse.

Date stones grow into an attractive palm, *Phoenix*

▼ A wide variety of seeds, pips and household vegetable scraps can be grown into attractive plants.

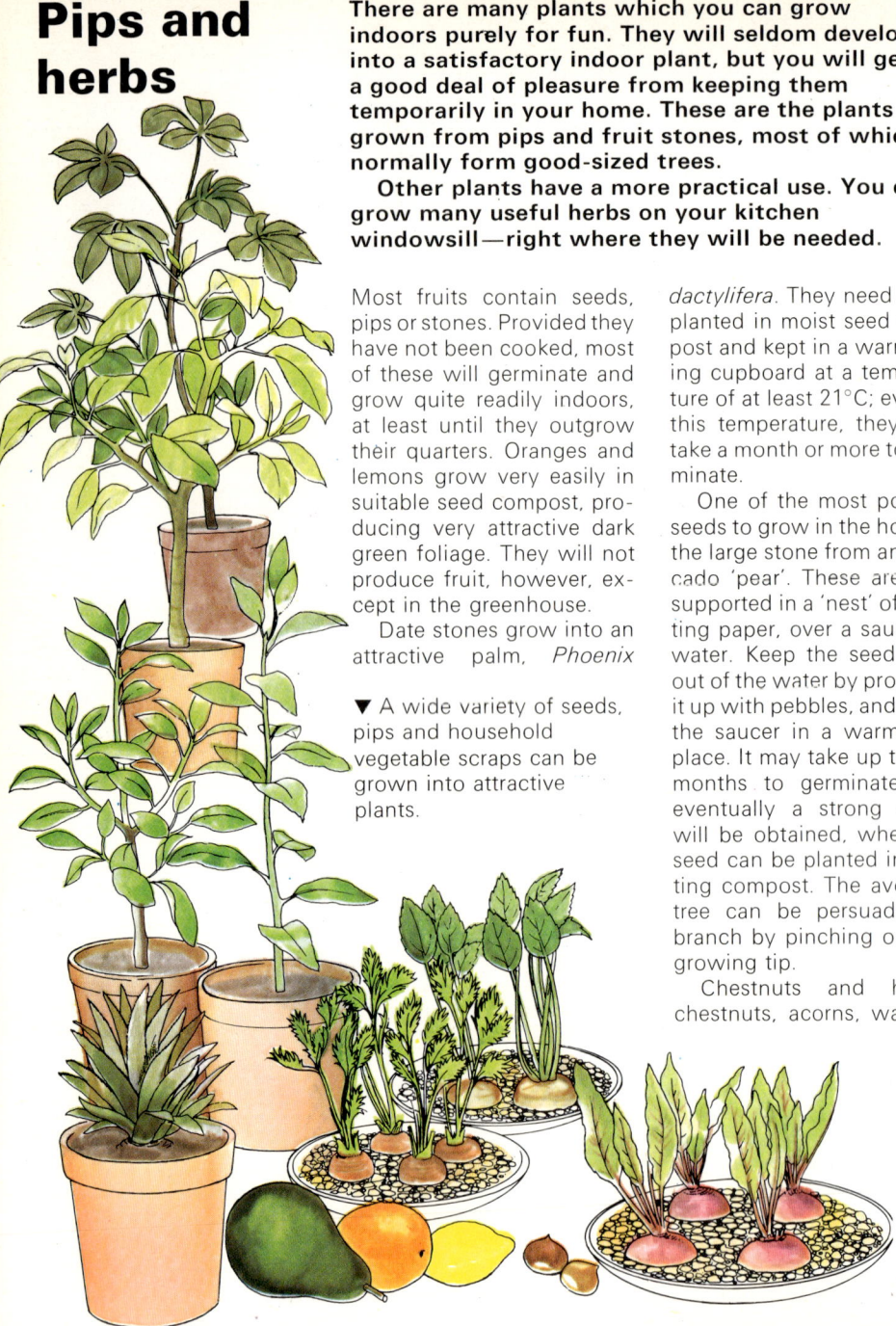

*dactylifera.* They need to be planted in moist seed compost and kept in a warm airing cupboard at a temperature of at least 21°C; even at this temperature, they may take a month or more to germinate.

One of the most popular seeds to grow in the home is the large stone from an avocado 'pear'. These are best supported in a 'nest' of blotting paper, over a saucer of water. Keep the seed itself out of the water by propping it up with pebbles, and place the saucer in a warm dark place. It may take up to two months to germinate, but eventually a strong shoot will be obtained, when the seed can be planted in potting compost. The avocado tree can be persuaded to branch by pinching out the growing tip.

Chestnuts and horse-chestnuts, acorns, walnuts,

and peach stones can also be germinated indoors, and transferred to the garden once they outgrow the home.

A number of kitchen scraps grow into intriguing indoor plants. Most people have seen a carrot 'fern', grown from the crown of a carrot placed in a saucer of water. Beetroots, parsnips and swedes can be grown in the same way.

Similarly, the spiky crown of a pineapple can be grown in a saucer of water, although it is better planted in potting compost, after letting the cut-off section dry out for a couple of days to minimize rotting. Once it has developed roots the pineapple can be treated like any other houseplant, and will develop into a large and very handsome plant with long spear-shaped leaves. After several years it may even produce fruit, if conditions are to its liking.

## Herbs

Most of the smaller types of herbs grow well indoors. In a trough about 50 cm long you can grow a selection of five or six different types in JI 2 compost. Rosemary, tarragon, parsley, thyme, marjoram and bay are all easy to grow from small plants bought in nurseries. They may be difficult to germinate from seed. Chives are useful and attractive in your herb trough. If you find the smell too pungent, place the pot of chives inside a deep covered glass jar, where the increased temperature and humidity will increase their growth rate.

▼ The kitchen windowsill is an ideal place to grow a trough of herbs, which can be picked quite fresh. Those most suitable for indoor cultivation are: Rosemary, Tarragon, Parsley, Thyme, Marjoram, Bay, Chives.

# Bottle gardens and plant cases

The Victorian fern cases allowed the most delicate plants to be grown in what would otherwise have been totally impossible conditions. Wardian cases, or terrariums as they are more generally known, are still available, but their main application nowadays is to overcome the damaging effects of the dry atmosphere in the modern home on more ordinary plants. You may wish to buy a modern terrarium, made from plastic or glass. Alternatively, there are several other ways in which you can produce attractive and novel displays using readily available materials.

Probably the easiest type is made from an aquarium. You can use an old cracked metal-framed glass aquarium, a goldfish bowl, or a modern one-piece plastic tank. You will also need a sheet of glass cut to fit exactly over the top of the tank. This type of terrarium is available in a variety of sizes, and is easy to plant and maintain.

Bottle gardens are more decorative but a little more difficult to set up. Large-mouthed sweet jars are useful for holding perhaps one or two specimen plants. Cider flagons and the clear glass demi-johns used by amateur wine-makers are a more convenient size, although they have a very narrow neck. Best of all are the huge glass carboys formerly used to transport chemicals. But clean these thoroughly before use.

You must take care in filling the bottle or terrarium. If you use an aquarium or wide-mouthed container, use the materials described below, but ignore those instructions appropriate only to bottle gardens.

## Bottle garden equipment

When you make up tools for cultivating your bottle garden be sure that they will not fall apart in use. It is difficult to retrieve dropped objects from the container. If you use a wide mouthed bottle, ordinary indoor plant tools are adequate. Otherwise make or adapt your own from wire and strips of wood. A long pair of tongs are particularly useful for planting and general maintenance.

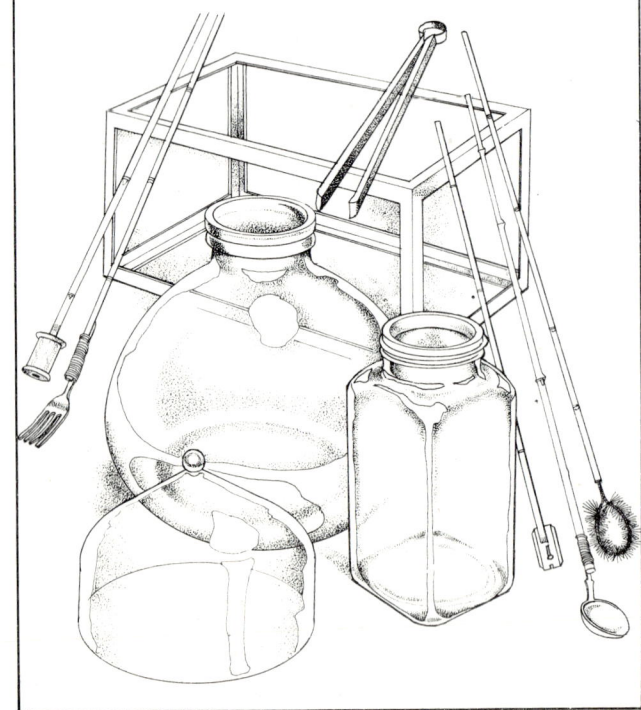

## Preparing the bottle garden

When you place compost in the bottle, it is important to keep it well clear of the sides, as it is difficult to remove adhering particles. Make up a roll of card, held together with adhesive tape, which reaches down into the bottle. You will be able to direct compost down this from an improvised paper funnel.

First you must cover the bottom of the container with about 2 cm of charcoal, which may be mixed with gravel, to provide adequate drainage. Cover this with about 6 cm of peat-based compost. This is easier to pour in while it is dry, but must be well soaked before any plants are added.

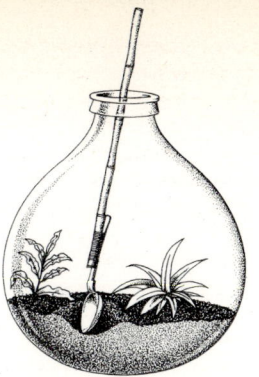

Depending on the diameter of the neck of your container, you may now need a specially improvised tool with which to reach in and dig out holes for your plants. An ordinary tablespoon tied to a stick is useful for this purpose. Gripping the plant is more difficult. You can make up long wooden tongs,

or bend a wire coat hanger to make a suitable hooked tool. Slip the plants in, root first, taking care not to damage the leaves, and place them into the holes you have dug. Now tamp down the compost around them firmly, using a cork or cotton-reel on the end of a stick or wire.

You will need to prune the plants occasionally, using a razor blade taped firmly to a long stick, and removing cut-off portions with your tongs. A plastic scouring pad attached to a piece of wire is also useful for cleaning green algae from the glass. This soon develops if your bottle garden is placed in a well-lit position.

And that's all there is to it! Add more water *only* if the compost seems to have dried out, and feed the plants with liquid fertilizer occasionally.

## The terrarium plants

Useful plants for the terrarium are: selaginella, acorus, codiaeum (*Croton*—use only small types), *Ficus pumila*, *Ficus radicans* 'Variegata', ferns, pileas, peperomias, ivies (small-leaved), maranta, saintpaulias, tradescantias, *Sansevieria hahnii*, small bromeliads—in fact, almost any moisture-loving plant which will not outgrow the container too rapidly.

# Display

If you are prepared to spend a lot of money, or have sufficient patience to wait while it grows, you can use a single specimen plant as a centre-piece. An enormous palm, monstera, or ficus makes a magnificent display without further adornment, but it is easier and more convenient to make up a display from a number of smaller plants.

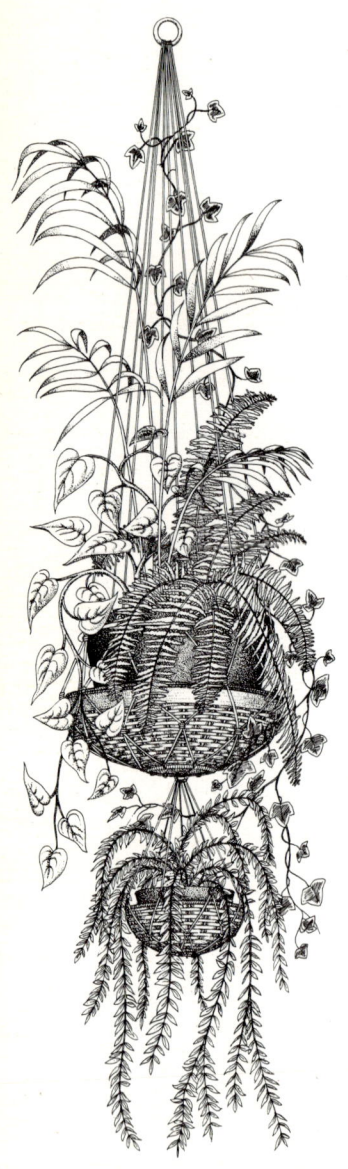

Most displays are made up in tubs or troughs. You can simply stand pots in the trough, but it is generally better to fill the trough with peat or some other absorbent material, like hydroleca, which encourages a moist atmosphere around the plant. Don't plant the specimens directly into the trough. Their roots will soon become intertwined, and you will be unable to replace plants without ruining the display.

The only exceptions are displays of cacti and succulents, which if carefully selected will be able to remain in the same container for years, owing to their slow growth rate.

Florists' displays, sold as table decorations, often combine flowering plants with foliage plants. They look very attractive but seldom last for long, as flowers are soon past their best, and the foliage plants rapidly outgrow the container.

## Some suggestions

For a balanced display, it is best to concentrate on one or two spectacular and brightly-coloured plants as the centre-piece, such as a dracaena, dieffenbachia, cordyline, or codiaeum. You can set these off by backing them with a tall-growing plant with contrasting but neutral-coloured foliage, such as *Rhoicissus rhomboidea* or *Philodendron scandens*, grown up a moss pole. In the foreground, try some low-growing plants and trailing plants to break up the harsh outline of the container. *Begonia rex* is available in almost limitless colour varieties, and peperomias and pileas form attractive low-growing mounds of variegated foliage. To trail over the edge of the container, perhaps a dense mat of pale-green helxine, variegated tradescantia or zebrina, or purple-leaved *Setcreasea purpurea*.

Do not overlook the possibilities of more unusual display methods. A particularly effective display technique is the use of hanging baskets, which show off trailing plants to perfection. The traditional types consist of a wire basket filled with sphagnum and peat compost, in which trailing pelargoniums and lobelia are grown, but modern types are often suspended from decorative macramé holders.

▶ A simple arrangement of trailing plants can transform a window into the centre-piece of a room.

# Problems, pests and diseases

How ever careful you are, sometimes you will be unlucky enough to lose a plant through ill-health, insect pests, or some less obvious cause. When you do, put it down to experience, and make sure you know what went wrong. Most diseases and pests only attack when a plant is already weakened from some other cause. A healthy plant can usually fight off disease, or tolerate a small number of insect pests. On the other hand, if your plant is one which is suitable for only temporary residence in the house, like the chrysanthemum, take care next time to adjust its stay indoors to the correct stage in its growing cycle.

### Overwatering

Too much water is the biggest single killer of indoor plants. Paradoxically, the symptoms of the over-watered plant are similar to those of drying out—the plant wilts. The immediate reaction is to add even more water, and the results are generally fatal to the plant. The cause is that the roots have suffocated in the airless compost, and rotted, so that they can no longer pump water up the stem to the leaves. The only possible remedy is to knock the plant out of its pot and let the soil-ball dry out for a couple of days, after which it can be repotted and watered cautiously—but it may be too late.

### Soil dryness

Plants are equipped to withstand drying out, up to a point. A plant wilting through lack of water will speedily recover once it has been given a good soaking, although delicate new foliage may be permanently damaged, and growth may be checked for a while. The remedy is obvious—don't let it happen.

### Sun scorch

Although a few plants like pelargoniums and cacti appreciate direct sunlight, this can be fatal for most indoor plants. The first warning signs are generally irregular dehydrated patches on the leaves. If the plant is not moved into shade, the damage will spread, eventually killing the whole plant.

### Cold water scorch

Some flowering plants such as saintpaulia, cyclamen, and sinningia (gloxinia) are easily damaged by cold water, which produces a peculiar mottled pattern on the leaves, and eventually causes rotting at the heart of the plant. This can be avoided by submerging the pot in lukewarm water, rather than using a watering can.

### Draughts

The effect of draughts on susceptible plants is rapid and dramatic. Soft-leaved plants like impatiens and coleus may suffer severe leaf droop, but more sensitive plants react by dropping off leaves without warning. Don't expose *any* plant to draughts, particularly in winter.

### Temperature changes

As with draughts, the first warning of severe temperature fluctuations is leaf drop. If the fluctuations are extensive, as in a plant stood on the windowsill of a heated room in winter time, most of the leaves may drop overnight. Behind the curtains, the temperature on the windowsill drops at night to little more than it is outside, and will quickly be fatal. Sudden increases in temperature are equally damaging, causing wilting. In either case, the plant can sometimes be saved by spraying it with cool water.

### Dry atmosphere

Leaves suffer first, turning brown at the tips and edges, and becoming dry and brittle. This is most likely to happen in the winter, when domestic heating dries the air in the room. Increase the local humidity about the plant by peat baths, water spraying, etc. Once the situation is under control, the damaged portions of the leaves can be trimmed off with scissors.

If you have a monstera, a warning sign is the loss of the natural slashes and holes in the newly developing leaves.

## Lack of light

All plants need light for healthy growth. If the conditions in their growing position are too dark, they will compensate by growing towards any available light, becoming leggy and straggly in the process. At the same time, loss of chlorophyll from the leaves makes them yellow and anaemic-looking, although the leaves do not actually drop off.

Conversely, a plant with adequate light is bushy and intensely coloured. Variegations and coloured foliage will fade to a pale green in poor light, as the plant manufactures extra chlorophyll in an attempt to make up the deficit. If you cannot place the plant in a better-lit situation, you might try artificial lighting.

## Unsuitable soil conditions

If the condition of the compost is incorrect your plant will show this by a change in leaf colour, and by checks in growth. Remember that a plant does not grow constantly throughout the year. The first and last leaves produced each year are much

| DISEASE | TREATMENT |
|---|---|
| **Mildew** Powdery or furry coating on leaves, stems, and buds. Encouraged by overcrowded displays. | *Dust affected plants twice a week with Benlate, sulphur, Thiram, or Karathane. Thereafter, dust every ten days to prevent recurrence. Thin out the plants and improve ventilation.* |
| **Botrytis** Fluffy greyish mould which first appears on dead material, then spreads to the living plant. Affects mostly cyclamen, saintpaulia, and sinningia. | *Do not leave dead leaves and fallen flowers in the pot. Lower the humidity and reduce watering, and spray once weekly with Benlate, for a total of 3 weeks. If plant dies, discard compost and sterilize pot.* |
| **Fungal spots** Soft brown patches affecting the leaves of ivies, dracaenas, dieffenbachia, and begonia. | *Remove infected leaves. Spray once weekly with Benlate, for a total of 3 weeks.* |
| **Damping off and root rots** Cuttings and young plants wilt and rot. Larger plants wilt or cease growth. | *Caused by use of contaminated compost. Water with Cheshunt Compound as a preventive measure. Avoid overwatering of mature plants. Water with Orthocide or Benomyl once every week for 3 weeks.* |

smaller than those produced when the plant is growing at its fastest in the spring and summer. The colour of these leaves also varies from time to time, quite naturally. But if previously healthy leaves start to look pale and yellowed, without actually dropping, some of the soil nutrients are probably exhausted. Iron or magnesium deficiency is the most likely cause, and this can be quickly remedied by a few sprayings with a foliar feed, followed by regular use of fertilizer on the compost. Repotting may be necessary and advisable. If your plant is one of the lime-hating types, check that you have not inadvertently potted it in ordinary compost, which will eventually cause this leaf discoloration.

# WHAT WENT WRONG?

**1. Slow growth** In the winter, your plants effectively halt their growth. If growth checks occur in the growing season, make sure you are providing adequate feed and water. Consider repotting.

**2. Pale and leggy** Plants kept too moist and too warm in the spring become leggy when they begin to grow.

**3. Wilting** Soil may be too dry, or conversely, may have been waterlogged for a prolonged period. Too much sunlight may also be the cause.

**4. Loss of variegation** When variegated leaves turn plain green, plants need more light.

**5. Leaf and bud drop** Sudden temperature changes, draughts, or moving pots to a different growing position. Can be caused by any environmental change.

**6. Yellowing leaves which drop off** Old leaves naturally turn yellow and drop off. When several are affected, overwatering or draughts may be the cause.

**7. Scorched leaves** Hot dry air causes scorching, as do excess sun, draughts, fertilizer splashes, and gas fumes.

**8. Stem and leaf rot** Caused by disease—usually resulting from overwatering and excess humidity.

**9. Yellow leaves which stay healthy** Due to use of lime and effects of hard water in plants which prefer acid or peaty composts.

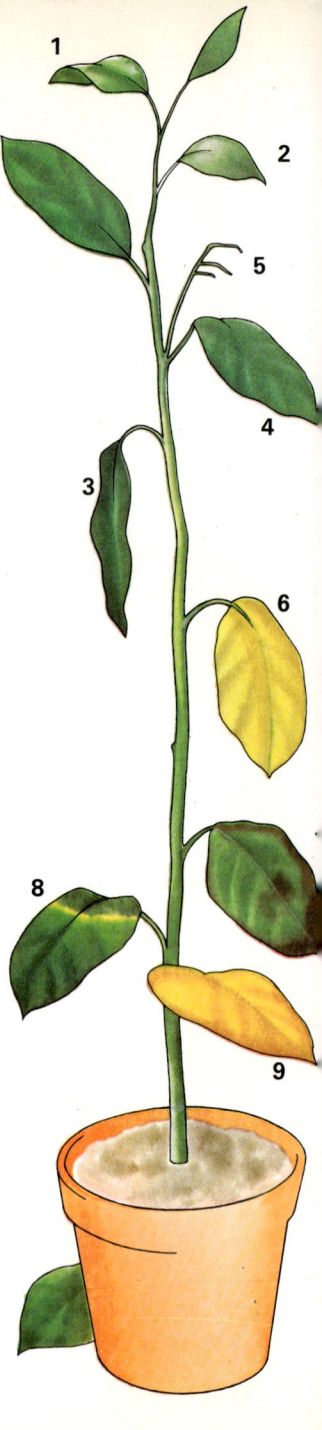

---

**Applying fungicides and pesticides**
Some plant health products can be applied directly to the compost by the watering can. Most are best applied directly to the foliage by a small mist sprayer. Make sure the chemical reaches the underside of the leaves and gets down into the crown of the plant, where pests can hide, and fungal diseases often start. Indoor plants do not always tolerate garden chemicals. Avoid these plant/pesticide combinations: BHC—kalanchoe, hydrangea; Dichlovos (usually sold as impregnated paper strips) for tradescantia, chrysanthemums; Dimethoate for chrysanthemum, calceolaria, cineraria, fuchsia, hydrangea, primula; Malathion for pileas, ferns.

# PESTS

1. **Aphids** or greenfly are common pests of the soft growing tips of indoor plants. Spray with derris, malathion, or Rogor as instructed on the bottle.

2. **Red spider mites** are tiny, almost invisible insects which cause yellowish mottling and shrivelling of leaves. They may also spin a fine web beneath the leaves. Found only in hot, dry conditions. Spray with derris, or use fumigant strips stuck into compost.

3. **Whiteflies** are tiny flying insects which suck sap from the leaves and cause yellowing. Repeated applications of malathion or derris may be necessary to control them.

4. **Scale insects** look like tiny brown limpets. They are killed by malathion, but their resistant bodies containing living eggs must be swabbed off with cotton wool soaked in methylated spirit, to prevent further outbreaks.

5. **Thrips** are tiny black insects which cause discoloured patches on the leaves, together with black specks. They are easily controlled with malathion or derris.

6. **Mealy bugs** are slow-moving pests with a greyish woolly covering. They attack the underside of leaves, and also get into the crown of the plant, where they are difficult to detect. Mealy bugs are resistant to many insecticides, and are best controlled by swabbing colonies with methylated spirit to remove the insects and their eggs.

# Glossary

**Adnate:** joined to another part of the plant.

**Adventitious:** parts of a plant growing from an unusual place, such as roots produced high up on the stem.

**Aerial root:** roots produced above ground level, as in monstera, philodendron, scindapsus, and other climbing and trailing plants.

**Alpine:** plant adapted to life in mountainous regions. Generally refers to dwarf species.

**Annual:** plant which completes its life cycle in one growing season from seed to seed and dies.

**Areole:** tuft of hairs found on cacti.

**Aroid:** plant belonging to the Araceae family, including monstera, philodendron, caladium and dieffenbachia.

**Axil:** joint at which a leaf stalk or petiole diverges from the stem. Source of axillary buds.

**Berry:** fleshy fruit containing seeds.

**Bicoloured:** flower in which two different colours are found in the same petal.

**Biennial:** plant which takes two years to complete its life cycle, growing from seed in the first year and maturing and dying in the following year.

**Bigeneric:** hybrid between plants of different genera, such as x *Fatshedera lizei*.

**Blind:** non-flowering, due to some accident, disease, or deficiency.

**Bracts:** modified leaves just below a flower. Often brightly coloured and resembling a flower, such as in poinsettia.

**Bromeliad:** spiky plant related to the pineapple.

**Bulb:** underground storage organ derived from a bud.

**Bulbil:** immature bulb, often budded off from mature bulb.

**Calcifuge:** plant which cannot tolerate lime.

**Calyx:** sepals or outer leaves surrounding a flower.

**Campanulate:** bell-shaped flower.

**Cheshunt Compound:** fungicidal chemical.

**Chlorophyll:** green pigment used by the plant in photosynthesis.

**Compost:** soil in which a plant is grown; also term for decomposed plant material.

**Container plant:** plant grown in a pot so it can be moved without causing damage to roots.

**Corm:** underground storage organ resembling a bulb, but consisting of a short, swollen stem.

**Corolla:** the petals of a flower.

**Crocks:** broken clay pots, bricks, or stones used to provide drainage in a planting container.

**Crown:** the point from which stems spread from the roots, usually just above soil level.

**Cultivar:** plant variety bred in cultivation.

**Cutting:** section of plant used to grow a new plant.

**Deciduous:** plant which drops its leaves at the end of the growing season.

**Dioecious:** plants with flowers of individual sexes.

**Division:** method of propagating plants which spread by underground shoots, stems, or roots.

**Dormant:** condition where plant stops growing, usually over the winter.

**Double:** flower with extra whorls of petals.

**Epiphytic:** plants adapted to living on tree branches or rocks; they are not parasites, however. Includes many orchids and bromeliads, and some ferns.

**Ericaceous:** plant resembling a heather.

**Evergreen:** plant retaining leaves throughout the year.

**F₁ hybrid:** artificially-bred hybrid between two dissimilar parents. Will not breed true.

**Family:** major botanical grouping of plants.

**Ferns:** primitive flowerless plants reproducing by spores.

**Forcing:** manipulating heat and light to cause growth or flowering out of season.

**Fungicide:** chemical to treat or prevent fungal diseases.

**Genus:** grouping of related plants.

**Germination:** initial development of a plant from a seed.

**Glabrous:** without hairs, smooth.

**Glaucus:** with a powdery 'bloom' on the surface.

**Grafting:** joining a section from one plant onto another. Sometimes carried out on cacti.

**Half-hardy:** plant which will survive outdoors in summer, but cannot tolerate frost.

**Hardening-off:** acclimatizing plants to indoor conditions, by gradually reducing growing temperatures.

**Hardy:** plant which can live outdoors throughout the year.

**Heel:** base of a cutting, tuber, or other material used for propagation.

**Herbaceous:** plant with non-woody stems.

**Humus:** decayed organic material.

**Hybrid:** strictly a cross between plants of differing species, but loosely used to describe a cross between two or more varieties.

**Inflorescence:** cluster of small flowers.

**Internode:** section of stem

between two nodes.
**Loam:** light fertile soil, rich in humus.
**Midrib:** large central vein in a leaf.
**Monoecious:** plant which carries only either male or female flowers.
**Mulch:** layer of organic material spread on compost to act as fertilizer, and to maintain soil humidity.
**Node:** joint in a stem from which leaves or sideshoots arise.
**Offset:** small plant produced by a mature plant. Can be detached and grown separately.
**Peat:** partially decayed remains of mosses and sedges; formed in bogs.
**Perennial:** plant which survives for more than two years.
**Petal:** flowerleaf.
**Petiole:** leaf stalk.
**Pinnate:** with leaflets on either side of the petiole.
**Pistil:** female organ of a flower, in which seeds are produced.
**Propagation:** method of reproducing plants.
**Procumbent:** lying loosely on the ground.
**Prostrate:** pressed tightly against the ground.
**Pseudo-bulb:** swollen stem of orchid storing water.
**Raceme:** spike-like, unbranched inflorescence.
**Rhizome:** underground stem growing horizontally and acting as a food store.
**Root-ball:** tightly packed mass of roots and compost.
**Rosette:** cluster of leaves radiating from the stem, e.g. bromeliads and many succulents.
**Runner:** shoot lying on the soil surface from which small plants are produced.
**Seed:** product of fertilization from which a new plant will grow.

**Self-coloured:** flower of a pure single colour.
**Sepal:** leaves protecting the petal, usually making up outer leaves of flowerbud.
**Sessile:** without a stalk.
**Shrub:** wood-stemmed plant which does not produce a trunk.
**Single:** flower with the usual number of petals, as opposed to double.
**Spadix:** thick and crowded spike of small flowers, as in *Anthurium.*
**Spathe:** fleshy and brightly coloured leaf surrounding a spadix.
**Species:** particular type of plant which normally breeds true.
**Sporangia:** sac-like structures on underside of fern fronds producing spores.
**Spores:** minute structures functioning as seeds by which ferns and other primitive plants reproduce.
**Sport:** a natural freak or mutation, which can be propagated vegetatively and will produce a new variety.
**Stamen:** male reproductive organ of a plant producing pollen.
**Standard:** plant grown with a

single tall stem.
**Stigma:** part of plant's female organs on which pollen is deposited.
**Stolon:** creeping stem.
**Stopping:** pinching-out growing tip to induce branching.
**Strike:** rooting a cutting.
**Succulent:** plant with fleshy leaves or stems which store water.
**Tender:** plant which cannot tolerate cold weather.
**Tendril:** fibre with which plants cling to a support.
**Terminal:** growing tip of plant.
**Terrestrial:** growing on the ground.
**Top dressing:** application of fertilizer or fresh compost to the soil surface.
**Tuber:** root acting as food store resembling bulb or rhizome.
**Variegated:** with leaves or petals patterned in contrasting colours.
**Variety:** small subdivision in the plant kingdom dividing a species.
**Whorl:** plant parts arranged in a ring.
**Xerophyte:** plant adapted to life under drought conditions.

| Pot name | Top diameter | | Depth | | Distance from top of pot to soil | |
|---|---|---|---|---|---|---|
| | cm | inches | cm | inches | cm | inches |
| Thumb | 6.5 | 2½ | 6.5 | 2½ | 1 | ½ |
| 60 | 7.5 | 3 | 9.0 | 3½ | 1 | ½ |
| 48 | 11.0 | 4½ | 12.5 | 5 | 1 | ½ |
| 32 | 15.0 | 6 | 15.0 | 6 | 2 | ¾ |
| 24 | 21.6 | 8½ | 20.0 | 8 | 2.5 | 1 |
| 16 | 24.0 | 9½ | 23.0 | 9 | 3 | 1¼ |
| 8 | 30.0 | 12 | 28.0 | 11 | 4 | 1½ |
| 4 | 37.5 | 15 | 33.0 | 13 | 5 | 2 |

# A-Z of indoor plants

JI 1 etc = John Innes No. 1 compost

Ease of growing
- ● easy
- ●● not so easy
- ●●● difficult

## 1 Acalypha hispida ●
Euphorbiaceae
Redhot Catstail, Chenille Plant
A very warm and humid atmosphere is needed for this shrub from New Guinea. Potting mixture should preferably be moisture retaining —a good loam, such as JI 1, or a peat-based compost, is best. It will succeed in a suitably warm and humid greenhouse but naturally grows to over 3 m so limiting its life under household cultivation. Drying out from direct sunlight should be avoided. The tail-like tassel of pink flowers may be up to 50 cm long. Pests include red spider mite and mealy bug. Propagate by cuttings.

## 2 Achimenes hybrids ●●
Gesneriaceae
These hybrids, developed from Central American and West Indian species, are herbaceous perennials with tuberous root-stocks. Potting mixture should preferably be moisture retaining but well drained, indeed the plants should be dried off in the autumn. Shade from direct sunlight. The plants are long flowering; the flowers may be white, pink, rose, red, violet, blue or spotted combinations of these colours. The plants vary in height,

50 cm being an average. Propagate by dividing the tubers when the plants are dried off.

**Adiantum see Ferns**
**Aechmea see Bromeliads**
**Aeonium see Succulents**
**Ananas see Bromeliads**

## 3 Anthurium scherzerianum ●●
Araceae
Flamingo Flower
Of the several hundred species of *Anthurium*, few are generally cultivated. The most suitable as a house plant is *A. scherzerianum*. It is from Central and South America. A moisture-retaining peat-based compost, preferably with some sphagnum moss, is most suitable provided it is well drained. Keep moist from mid-autumn to spring and water freely. During the winter keep warm, about 13°C, but not in a hot, dry position. The scarlet heart-shaped flowers, with a central whitish 'tail', appear from spring to autumn. Grows up to 30 cm. Aphids are the main pest and may be very troublesome. Propagate by division in spring, making sure that each division has a growing point and roots.

## 4 Aphelandra squarrosa ●●●
Acanthaceae
Zebra plant
A herbaceous perennial from Brazil, useful both for the yellow flowers and evergreen leaves with white stripes of most varieties such as 'Louisae'. Flowers late summer into autumn and grows up to about 60 cm high with a spread of about 30 cm. Grow in a fairly light place and shade from strong sunlight. Needs plenty of water when growing so use a moisture-retentive

mixture, such as a peat-based compost. Keep drier during the winter months but do not allow it to dry out completely. Cut back the plants after flowering. The main pest is scale insect. Propagate in spring or summer using cuttings from near the base.

**Aporocactus see Cactus**

## 5 Araucaria excelsa ●
Araucariaceae
Norfolk Island Pine
Probably the best known plant of the genus is *A. araucana*, the Monkey Puzzle. The Norfolk Island Pine is, however, possibly the best house plant of its type. Though not a true conifer, it looks rather like a more graceful Christmas tree and under home cultivation it may grow to 2 m. JI 2 compost is suitable. The plant should be kept watered and fed from spring to autumn, but just moist for the rest of the year. A light and well ventilated position is best; in summer the plant may be kept outdoors. Usually fairly free of pests and diseases. Propagate by seeds in March or cuttings from young shoots.

**5**  **6**

**7a**  **7b**  **9**

## 6 Asparagus ●
Liliaceae
The two species which make
the best house plants are
*Asparagus densiflorus*
'Sprengeri', often known as
*A. sprengeri*, and *A. setaceus*,
the Asparagus Fern, which is
also known as *A. plumosus*
(6). Though it belongs to the
lily family, the flowers are
insignificant and they are
grown for their foliage. This is
particularly fine and feathery in
the Asparagus Fern, but mature
plants tend to climb. On the
other hand 'Sprengeri' will
sprawl, the stems falling down
over the pot edge making a
plant more than 1 m across.
Both plants sometimes produce
red berries.
   They both need well lit
positions but preferably not
direct sunlight. JI 2 is suitable
for growing them in. Plants
bought in 7.5-cm (3-in) pots
will usually have to be potted-
up into 10-cm (4-in) pots or,
in the case of 'Sprengeri', may
be grown in a hanging basket.
Change the soil annually, in
late spring, and put into a
larger pot if necessary. Keep
well watered in warm weather
but just moist through the

winter. Keep free of frost. A
liquid feed about every
fortnight when growing is
beneficial in summer. Red
spider mite and scale insects
are the main pests but the
plants are generally disease-
free. Plants may be raised from
seed or by dividing larger
plants in spring.

## 7 Aspidistra elatior ●
Liliaceae
The aspidistra is a member of
the lily family and is also
known as *A. lurida* (7a). It is
probably one of the most
famous of all house plants and
indeed it is a very good one. A
particularly fine looking
aspidistra has creamy-white
striped variegated leaves (7b).
Extremely tolerant of house
conditions, they will of course
suffer if they are too dried out,
overwatered or put in a very
draughty position. The arching
leaves may grow about 50 cm
long so that the spread is over
1 m, though the height is
considerably less. JI 2, or a
soilless equivalent, is suitable.
Keep well watered in summer,
just moist in winter when they
should preferably be kept frost-
free, though they are hardy.
Repot about every two years
and pot-on, up to a 25-cm
(10-in) pot for large plants. A
weak liquid feed is beneficial
every month in summer. Main
pests are red spider mite and
scale insects. Disease is
generally absent, though
browning of leaves may be
caused by bad conditions such
as overwatering and bad

drainage. Propagate by dividing
plants in spring.

**Asplenium** see **Ferns**

**Azalea** see **Rhododendron**

## 8 Begonia ●
Begoniaceae
This is a large genus of plants,
a few of which may be grown
as house plants. These include
foliage plants which may be
grown indoors all the year
round and flowering plants
which are brought into the
house for their flowering
period.
1 Foliage begonias. The best
plants are *Begonia masoniana*,
Iron Cross begonia (8a) and
hybrids and varieties of *B. rex*
(8b). The rex varieties have
many colour forms and include
shades of green, silver, red,
purple, pink and brown often
mixed on the leaves. These
grow up to 30 cm high and
arise from rhizomatous roots.
Other begonias with attractive
leaves are *B. boweri* (8c), the
Eyelash begonia, with leaves
dotted dark brown around the
margins and small white to
pale pink flowers in spring;
*B. maculata* (8d) has spotted
leaves and the silver haired
*B. metallica* (8e) with metallic
green leaves and reddish veins
is a good house plant.
2 Flowering begonias. The two
main forms grown in the house
are varieties of *B.* x
*tuberhybrida*, tuberous rooted
begonias, and *B. semperflorens*
with fibrous roots. The
tuberhybrida begonias have
flowers in brilliant oranges,

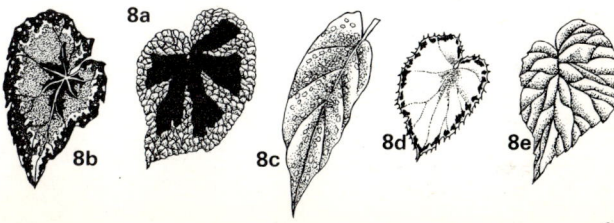

**8a**  **8b**  **8c**  **8d**  **8e**

reds, yellows and pinks and have fairly large leaves. They grow up to 60 cm high. The Pendula types also have similar leaves and flowers which hang down and are suitable for hanging baskets. The semperflorens types have small, glossy, round leaves and flowers in shades of pink, red and also white. They grow up to 30 cm high.

All begonias require a moisture-retaining but well drained soil; they will not flourish if too wet or too dry. JI 2, or a peat-based soilless compost, is suitable. They need plenty of light but the foliage and tuberous types should be shaded from direct sunlight, although the semperflorens will tolerate some. The tuberous begonias die down during winter and should be kept at 7 to 10°C, the others at about 10 to 13°C. These may have leaves but they will be resting before coming into flower later. Begonias are fairly pest-free but may be attacked by root weevils and leaf eelworms. The main diseases are various fungi —grey mould, powdery mildew and damping off which may attack young plants.

Propagate the tuberous begonias by dividing the tubers when they are dormant, and making sure each piece has an 'eye' to grow up from. The foliage begonias have rhizomes which may be divided. The semperflorens plants may be divided or grown from seed sown in spring or propagated from cuttings at any time of the year.

1

2

3

### 9 Beloperone guttata ●
Acanthaceae
Shrimp Plant
This small, shrubby plant comes from Mexico. JI 3, or an equivalent soilless compost, is suitable for repotting or

potting-on cuttings in early spring using a 12.5- or 15-cm (5- or 6-in) pot. When repotting a plant grown through the previous year, it is best to cut it well back to induce a compact bushy specimen. Some also advocate pinching out the first few flower buds to encourage more to form. A well grown plant will reach over 40 cm high and have a similar spread. Keep well watered from mid-spring to early winter and feed about every two weeks; in winter keep moist and at about 7°C. Shade from strong sunlight, but a light, cool position will help the flowers to last. Pests generally do not cause a problem and leaf troubles are more likely to be caused by incorrect watering or draughts than fungal disease. Propagate by cuttings in early spring. (See page 65 for illustration.)

### Billbergia see Bromeliads

### 10 Bromeliads ●—●●●
Bromeliaceae
Pineapple family
This is a very large family with well over 1000 species from South, Central and southern North America, the Caribbean islands and the West Indies.

21

22

23

15

Those grown do best in a warm and humid greenhouse but most may be brought in and grown in the house for a while. Good light is important and preferably rain rather than tap water should be used. Those plants forming rosettes of leaves should have the central cup kept filled and some moisture in the soil. Nutrients are best supplied by rather weak, liquid feeds, applied as foliar feeds or to the soil. A 12.5-cm (5-in) pot is usually sufficient but larger plants may need up to 17.5-cm (7-in) pots. JI 1 or 2, with an additional handful of peat per pot mixed in, or a loam-free compost, is suitable. When growing keep the soil watered, when dormant just moist. In a dry atmosphere, however, the plants should be regularly sprayed to improve humidity. They are generally free of pests and diseases but waterlogging will rot them.

Propagation by offsets, cut off near the base when nearly half the size of the parent plant, is quicker than by seeds. Pineapples may also be grown from the crown of leaves cut from the fruit top.

*Aechmea fasciata*, Urn Plant, is often sold as *Aechmea*

*rhodocyanea*. It has broad, upright leaves banded in shades of grey-green to about 60 cm high. From the central 'urn' a pink flower spike arises with a terminal head of pink bracts from which protrude vivid blue flowers. About 10°C is a reasonable winter temperature.

*Ananas comosus*, Pineapple, and *Ananas sagenaria*, Wild Pineapple, both have variegated forms which are rather similar with cream to yellow bands running the length of the leaves. They are not likely to produce fruit except under greenhouse conditions. *A. comosus* was formerly known as *A. sativus* and *A. sagenaria* as *A. bracteatus*.

*Billbergia nutans*, Angel Tears, gets its English name from the gracefully drooping flowerheads. An easy plant to keep, this is one of the bromeliads grown for its flowers rather than its upright, green leaves which are about 45 cm long. The flowerspike, held on a slender stem, is conspicuous with its pink bracts from which hang the yellowish-green, blue-margined flowers with bright yellow stamens.

▲ Bromeliads are mainly grown for their variously coloured, rosette-forming leaves and often brilliantly hued flower bracts.

1 *Aechmea fasciata*
2 *A. fulgens* 'Discolor'
3 *A. macracantha*
4 *A. chantinii*
5 *Ananas comosus*
6 *A. comosus* 'Variegatus'
7 *A. comosus* 'Striatus'
8 *Billbergia nutans*
9 *Cryptanthus acaulis*

*Cryptanthus* species do not form the usual storage 'cups' although the leaves grow in a rosette. Most grow up to 10 cm and some, such as *C. bromelioides*, to over 30 cm. They are all grown for their strongly marked leaves, some with horizontal bands of colour and others with the variegations running along the leaves. Humid, shady but warm areas of the home are best for these fairly easy house plants.

*Guzmania lingulata* forms a water-holding rosette with leaves 45 cm long. The striking bracts of vivid crimson are longer lasting than the pale yellowish flowers and arise on a 30-cm stem.

*Neoregelia* and *Nidularium* are two bromeliad genera with

10 *C. bivittatus*
11 *C. zonatus*
12 *C. bivittatus* 'Roseo-pictus'
13 *C. bromelioides* 'Tricolor'
14 *C. fosterianus*
15 *Guzmania lingulata*
16 *Neoregelia carolinae* 'Tricolor'
17 *Neoregelia marechalii*
18 *Neoregelia spectabilis*
19 *Nidularium innocentii*
20 *Tillandsia lindenii*
21 *Vriesea splendens*
22 *V. fenestralis*
23 *V. hieroglyphica*

rather similar requirements and appearance. They are 'cup' forming and require water in these reservoirs. They also need warm conditions. *Neoregelia carolinae* 'Tricolor' is spectacular when it changes

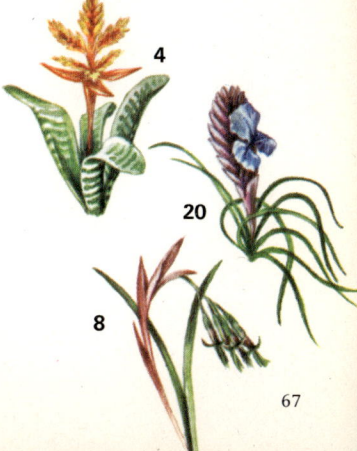

colour at flowering time. The normally shining green leaves, with a central, creamy stripe, become suffused with pink and the central 'cup' and leaves become rich red. *N. spectabilis* has red tips to its 30 cm leaves which, lying fairly flat, give the plant a spread of about 60 cm. The central leaves turn red at flowering time. *Nidularium innocentii* and *N. fulgens* have orange-red and scarlet centres to their rosettes respectively.

*Tillandsia* is a genus with only a few of its several hundred species in cultivation. They are not good house plants but may come as a gift. They all need very warm and humid greenhouse conditions to thrive. These are three species generally available: *Tillandsia cyanea*, Pink Quill, has narrow, green leaves and an unusual flowerhead of overlapping bracts, rosy hued when the lilac-blue flowers appear; *T. lindenii*, also known as *T. lindeniana*, Blue-flowered Torch, which has green leaves, brownish-purple below, and a flowerhead with rose-coloured bracts from which violet-blue flowers appear; *T. usneoides*, Spanish Moss, is quite unlike the other bromeliads described, having trailing stems from which thin, grey leaves up to 8 cm long arise—the yellowish flowers appear from the leaf axils in summer.

*Vriesea splendens*, Flaming Sword, is most attractive. The leaves are rather like the *Aechmea*, broad, green and banded with brownish-purple, and up to 40 cm long. The lower spike may reach nearly 1 m, the last 30 cm or so being the flowerhead of red bracts from which protrude the small, yellow flowers.

**Bryophyllum** see **Succulents**

**11 Cacti** ●—●●
Cactaceae
Natives of the Americas, most cacti available for growing in the house fall into two types.
1 Prickly types. These have round or cylindrical stems covered with spines and hooks. The dwarf and slow growing species and varieties are more suitable for the home. Many flower quite readily and in brilliant colours. They need warmth, light and moisture but, like many other plants, careful watering is necessary or they will rot. Keep the pot only just moist. The soil balance should be fairly neutral—neither too acid nor too alkaline. A good growing medium comprises equal parts of a gritty compost, sharp sand, ground brick or tile pieces, and peat and loam, which has not had any leafmould or manure for some time. Do not use fertilizer for 9 to 12 months, after which a high-potash, liquid feed may bc used. The winter temperature should not fall below about 4°C.

*Aporocactus flagelliformis*, Rat's-tail Cactus (11a), should

11b 11d 11g

11e 11c 11j 11h

be cultivated as for an epiphytic cactus. Its long trailing stems, 30 to 40 cm long, make it suitable for hanging pots or baskets. Shocking pink flowers grow up to 5 cm long and 2.5 cm across in spring.

*Cephalocereus senilis*, Old Man Cactus (11b), is slow growing and a good house cactus. The English name comes from the long hairs which drape round the stem. Yellow flowers appear in summer.

*Chamaecereus silvestrii*, Peanut Cactus (11c), gets its English name from the stubby stems, up to 8 cm long by 1.5 cm across. These easily break off and may be planted individually. The orange-red trumpet flowers grow to about 5 cm long.

*Echinocereus* species do not branch out from buds on the surface but form buds which burst out from within the plant. Summer flowering. Several species are available: *E.*

*engelmannii*, purple-red flowers; *E. knippelianus* (11d), rosy-violet inside and brownish outside the flowers; *E. pentalophus*, rosy-pink flowers; *E. scheeri*, pink flowers.

*Echinopsis*, Sea Urchin Cactus, gets both its botanic and its English names from the round spiny form of its stem, on which large flowers form. Good plants include *E. eyriesii* (11e), white flowers; *E. multiplex*, scented, pink flowers; *E. rhodotricha*, grows to over 60 cm high, white flowers.

*Mammillaria* species are globular to cylindrical in shape. *M. bocasana*, Powder Puff, grows about 15 cm high with cream flowers, an easy plant to grow; *M. elegans* has purple-tinged, red flowers; *M. hahniana*, Old Lady Mammillaria, is covered with silky-white spines and, when flowering, crimson flowers; *M. zeilmanniana* (11f) produces offsets which may be

individually potted-up and has yellow-throated, mauve flowers.

*Notocactus tubularis* (11g) forms a rather globular stem about 10 cm high and has yellow flowers in early summer.

*Opuntia*, Prickly Pear, has many attractive species and varieties. Most have a typical round, flattish stem with similar pad-like branches and they all flower in summer: *O. humilis* may grow to 1 m, yellow flowers tinged red; *O. microdasys*, Bunny Ears (11h), also grows to 1 m and has its pads covered with yellowish tufts and yellow flowers; *O. salmiana*, lower growing at about 50 cm, has rounder stems and yellow flowers; *O. verschaffeltii*, grows to about 30 cm with roundish stems and fiery orange flowers.

*Parodia penicillata* (11i) is another round-stemmed cactus with red flowers.

*Rebutia* has several free-flowering species including *R. aureiflora*, about 5 cm high with yellow flowers in spring; *R. miniscula*, up to 4 cm high with bright red flowers in summer; *R. miniscula violaciflora*, also known as *R. violaciflora*, has pinkish-lilac flowers; *R. xanthocarpa*, about 5 cm high, has reddish flowers.
2 Epiphytic types. These usually have thick, flattish and rather leaf-like stems with occasional little tufts of spines and often brilliant flowers. They need a richer compost than the prickly types; about three parts good loam, six parts leafmould and one part of drainage material—sharp sand or brick—is a good basic mixture. Add to this a little bone-meal and a trace of sulphate of potash. The balance of the compost should be neutral to slightly acid, since some of this type do not like

11i

11k

11a

lime. They will flourish in cool and slightly shaded conditions and require regular watering in the growing season, being kept just moist at other times. The winter temperature should not fall below about 2°C.

*Epiphyllum* has several excellent hybrids and some interesting species: *E. anguliger* is grown for its attractive flat stems, somewhat resembling the sword of a swordfish, and for its richly scented, white flowers; *E. cooperi*, not a true species, has very large, white, scented flowers. Hybrids include 'Carl von Nicolai', pink; 'Eastern Trance', large, pink; 'London Gaiety', two-tone pink; 'London Glory', large, orange-red and magenta; 'London Majestic', large, scented, mauve; 'London Surprise', large, scented, orange; 'Padre', large pink and flowering at odd times; 'Reward', large, yellow; 'Thalia', orange-red.

*Rhipsalidopsis* species need an acid compost. They are free-flowering and easy plants to grow. *R. gaertneri*, Easter Cactus (11j), also known as *Schlumbergera gaertneri*, has short stems 5 to 8 cm long and scarlet flowers in late spring; *R. rosea* has shorter stems and pink flowers, also in late spring.

Schlumbergera are somewhat similar to rhipsalidopsis. *S. truncata* and some hybrids are known as Christmas Cacti. *S. truncata*, also known as *S. russelliana* and *Zygocactus truncata*, has red flowers; *S. x buckleyi*, magenta flowers; 'Christmas Joy', scarlet-red flowers; 'Winter Tales', pink-flushed flowers.

Both types will need repotting every few years, replacing all the soil—shake the old soil gently out of the roots. The same pot may be

used again, or a slightly larger one may be required, the aim being to allow a little room for further growth in the two or three years before the next repotting. The best time is at the beginning of the growing season.

Propagation is by seed, grafting—for some forms of the prickly type—and cuttings, especially for the second type. Some cacti also produce offsets which may be removed and potted-up individually.

The main pests of cacti are probably mealy bugs, both stem and root types. Other typical indoor pests may also attack if present. Cacti are usually free of diseases—rot caused by overwatering or bad drainage is the most likely.

## 12 Calceolaria hybrids ●
Scrophulariaceae
Slipperwort
These colourful hybrids have been developed from South American species. They are annuals raised from seed sown in early summer. They may be grown in a sheltered position outdoors such as an open frame or box of similar depth. Bring indoors in early autumn and place in a cool position. Pot them on, using a loam-based compost such as John Innes, until they are in their final pots about mid-winter. They vary in height from 20 to 45 cm. Pests include whitefly and leaf hopper. Generally they are disease-free.

## 13 Campanula isophylla ●
Campanulaceae
Bellflower
This delightful plant from Italy has blue star-shaped flowers although there is a white variety. Since their height is about 15 cm but the spread up to about 1 m, hanging baskets or other positions from which the plants may trail or sprawl are suitable. Best grown in a potting mixture such as John Innes, they thrive in warm, light conditions. Propagate in spring by cuttings or division. Pests include whitefly and red spider mite. They are generally disease-free.

## 14 Capsicum ●
Solanaceae
Red Pepper
The ornamental peppers are grown for their brightly coloured fruits. Most are hybrids of a tropical species which includes *C. annuum* and *C. frutescens*.

They are grown as annuals needing to be replaced each year. Depending on size they are best in 12.5- to 20-cm (5- to 8-in) pots with a fairly rich, moisture-retentive compost. Watering by spraying is preferable. Feed with liquid fertilizer from when the fruit appears until it is finally coloured. A light, airy position is best. Propagate by seed sown in spring and keep at about 16°C. Start the individual plants off, when large enough to handle, in 7.5-cm (3-in) pots of JI 1. Pests include greenfly, which may be difficult to check, and red spider mite. Generally disease-free.

Varieties include 'Fiesta', (14a), 22 cm, bushy, white fruit turns red; 'Fips' (14b), 17 cm, pale green fruit changes through orange to deep red; 'Fireworks', 15 cm, upright, conical fruit changes from white to red; 'Variegata', 25 cm, fruit turns red, variegated white, green and purple foliage.

**Cephalocereus senilis** see **Cacti**

### 15 Ceropegia woodii ●
Asclepiadaceae
String of Hearts
This plant, originally from South Africa, is best displayed in a position which allows its long stems to hang down. They are festooned with fleshy heart-shaped leaves which are a mottled silver and green on their upper surface and purple beneath. In summer small, unusual, purple flowers appear. A light position is best. The plant will tolerate a wide range of temperature, doing best in some warmth. Keep just moist. Propagation is by new tubers which grow on the trailing stems. Start these in a 7.5-cm (3-in) pot using JI 2 and pot-up as necessary. Usually pest- and disease-free.

**Chamaecereus silvestrii** see **Cacti**

17a

17b

### 16 Chlorophytum ●
Liliaceae
Spider Plant
Decorative foliage plant of the lily family from South Africa. The most popular form is the green-leafed *C. capense*, also known as *C. elatum*. The variegated form, 'Variegatum', has a white stripe running down the centre of each leaf. Another Spider Plant has white-edged leaves. They are best when their stems, which may reach 2 m, trail down, showing off the new plantlets which form along them. They are tolerant of quite low temperatures and some shade as well as some neglect and sunshine. Propagate by starting the plantlets off in small pots of JI 2 or a soilless equivalent. As they grow, pot-on until they are in a 20- to 22.5-cm (8- to 9-in) pot. Feed lightly during the growing season. Generally pest-free, but the leaf tips may turn brown perhaps through overwatering.

### 17 Chrysanthemum ●
Compositae
This relative of the daisy is now available as a short-term house plant in many splendid colours and forms (17a and 17b). Long-term plants require a greenhouse. The forms dealt with here are those usually bought in a pot large enough to see them through their flowering period when they are then generally

discarded. During this time their requirements are few. They need plenty of water and an occasional feed of dilute liquid fertilizer. They are tolerant of most house conditions except dry ones. Such plants are specially treated so that they remain dwarf. There are usually several plants to a pot to give an impression of bushiness. Plants grown-on for another year, or propagated from them, are unlikely to retain the same characteristics.

**Cineraria** see **Senecio**

### 18 Cissus antarctica ●
Vitaceae
Kangaroo Vine
This Australian plant is grown as a climber and for its shiny

18

green, heart-shaped leaves. It will reach more than 2 m in a 15-cm (6-in) pot of soilless compost or JI 2. Canes, or other supports, are needed and it will require tying up occasionally. Keep in a well lit position with plenty of water in the growing season and use a liquid fertilizer feed every two or three weeks. Keep above 7°C in winter. Greenfly is the most probable pest; red spider mite and mealy bugs might also occur. Disease is usually absent, though leaf-fall or browning may be caused by overwatering.

**19 Citrus mitis** ●
Rutaceae
Calamondin Orange
The brilliant orange fruits are the main attraction of this dark-leaved bush from the Philippines. The fruit is bitter but may be eaten. The white flowers are also attractive and fragrant. It will grow to more than 45 cm high. Start in JI 2 and as you pot-up to a final 20- to 25-cm (8- to 10-in) pot size use JI 3. Water freely during the summer and keep just moist at other times, for this is an all-the-year-round plant. Some warmth is required in winter, but below 13°C.

Pests include scale insect and also mealy bug. Overwatering may cause leaf-fall. Propagate by cuttings in late summer, starting them off after rooting in 7.5-cm (3-in) pots. Other *Citrus* species may be grown from pips but are not long-term house plants. See page 52.

**20 Clivia miniata** ●
Amaryllidaceae
Kaffir Lily

Originally from South Africa, this is a most rewarding house plant. Light orange to red, trumpet-shaped flowers appear from spring to late summer, and the arching strap-like leaves reach about 45 cm high. Start in 12.5-cm (5-in) pots and pot-on as needed until they are in 30-cm (12-in) pots. Keep well watered when growing, but only just moist during winter. A warm position is best, though the minimum winter temperature may go as low as nearly 4°C. Good light, but not direct sunlight, is suitable. Pests are usually confined to mealy bugs; disease is not common. Propagate by division in spring; this is tricky as the roots become very tangled and should not be broken if this can be avoided. Seed sown singly in 7.5-cm (3-in) pots as soon as available produces variable plants—truly pot luck.

**21 Codiaeum variegatum** ● ● ●
Euphorbiaceae
Croton
The variety of this Malaysian plant which is so well known for its brilliant leaves is called *pictum*. There are many colour forms in orange, yellow, green and crimson, splashed, dotted or striped. Different forms may have leaves of various shapes to add to the interest. It is, however, a difficult plant to grow. Positioning is the key to success. It needs good light but not direct sunlight, a humid atmosphere and a constant temperature which in winter should not fall below 16°C. Draughts, dryness or a too damp, waterlogging soil will all cause trouble. A soilless compost or JI 2 (JI 3 if the plant is large) is suitable. Keep moist—only just in winter— and use warmed water of

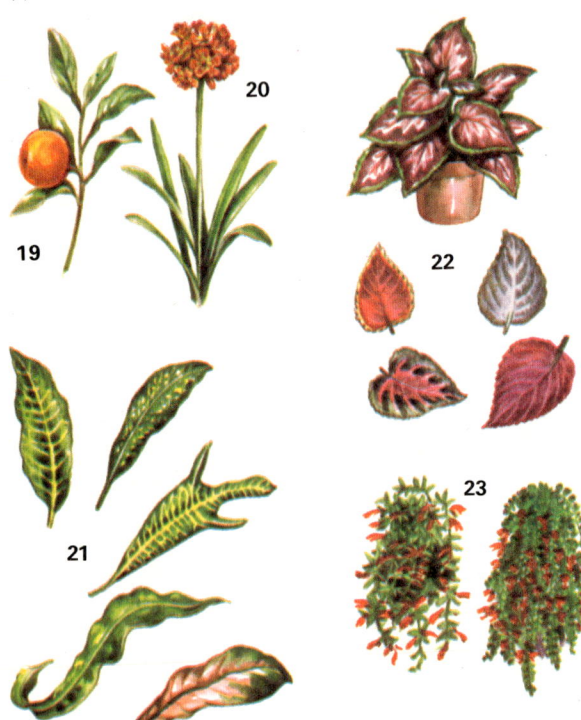

72

▶ Some of the brilliant colour range of coleus' leaves are shown here. Other forms have twisted and heavily cut leaves as well.

about 16°C. Water straight from the tap may well be too cold. In spring, pot into a larger pot if necessary and in summer feed every week or so with a dilute liquid fertilizer. Pests include scale insect and also mealy bugs and red spider mite; usually disease-free. Propagate by cuttings, 6 to 8 cm long, spring to early summer. The cut will bleed so dab it with paper tissue, or dip it into powdered charcoal, to dry before insertion in an equal parts mixture of sharp sand and peat. Temperature should be 24°C. Cover with a polythene bag or place in a propagator to keep it humid.

## 22 Coleus blumei ●●
Labiatae
Usually grown as an annual for its brilliant foliage, the cultivated varieties of this Javanese plant may be kept from year to year but take some trouble to look after. Almost any position in the house is suitable. But radiators, where plants tend to dry out too quickly, and too shady places, where leaf colour will be poor, should be avoided. Leaf colours will also suffer in winter. JI 2 is a suitable compost. Pot-on when required until a maximum pot size of 20 cm (8 in) is reached. Pinch out growing shoots before flowers develop, to improve bushiness, and restrict height to about 45 cm. Pests include mealy bugs and whitefly. Generally disease-free. Propagate by seeds sown in mid-winter, or by cuttings taken from late summer or, if kept over winter, in late spring.

## 23 Columnea ●●
Excellent plants for hanging baskets or suspended pots; the trailing stems, 60 cm to 2 m long, with their close-set leaves and brilliant, horizontal flowers, may then be seen to best advantage. The flowers range in colour from deep yellow to vermilion or brownish-red, and are 4 to 8 cm long. The cultivated species mainly come from Costa Rica and Mexico. A humid, warm atmosphere and a potting mixture comprising equal parts of sphagnum moss and JI 2 or JI 3 are required. Winter temperature should be about 16°C. Rarely troubled by pests and diseases. Propagate by cuttings in the summer. The hybrid *C. x banksii* has vermilion flowers from winter to spring; *C. gloriosa*, red and yellow flowers, mainly winter to spring, and in the variety 'Purpurea' dark purple-to-

copper leaves; *C. microphylla*, scarlet and yellow flowers, winter to spring; *C. schiediana*, red and yellow flowers, spring to summer.

## 24 Cordyline and Dracaena ●●
Liliaceae
These two genera of the lily family are so often confused that it seems best to treat them together here. The cordylines come from Australasia and Asia, the dracaenas from Africa and the Canaries. Dracaenas have more showy variegated leaves, cordylines are more palm-like and have sword-like leaves. Both should be grown in JI 2 when young and JI 3 as they mature. They need a winter temperature of 10 to 13°C, except *C. australis* and *D. draco* which will tolerate about 7°C. Large plants will require 15- to 22.5-cm (6- to 9-in)

pots. Fairly pest-free, but root mealy bugs and scale insects may occur. The main disease is leaf spot. Propagate by removing basal shoots and suckers in spring or take cuttings of old stems about 8 cm long. When rooted plant up into 7.5- to 10-cm (3- to 4-in) pots of JI 1 or JI 2.

**Crassula** see **Succulents**

### 25 Crocus ● ●
Iridaceae
Crocuses are not plants to last in the house and after flowering they should be discarded or planted out. A cold position is needed to ensure flowerbud development. Pot the corms in autumn, about eight to a 15-cm pot, using JI 1 or a soilless equivalent. If they cannot be planted outside under sand, peat, or ashes if available, put them in a cold room in the dark. Wait until the shoots are about 3 cm, then bring into a light, but still cold, position. Keep moist but not soaking.

### 26 Cyclamen persicum hybrids ● ●
Primulaceae
These hybrids, members of the primrose family, are often grown, not only for their lovely flowers, but also for their beautifully marked leaves. The original wild plant came from the East Mediterranean. Growing from 13 to 25 cm high, larger plants will need 15-cm (6-in) pots of JI 2. Keep moist and maintain humidity until they are growing by standing the pots on pebbles in a bowl of water. They require good light but not direct sunlight. In winter the temperature should be about 16°C. When growth and flowering are over in summer, put them in a north-facing

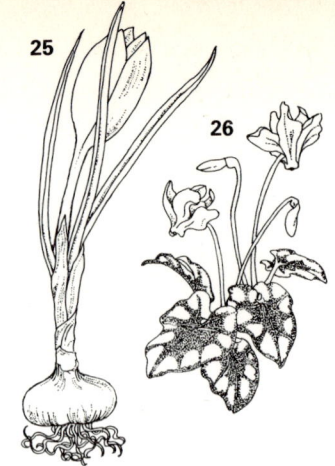

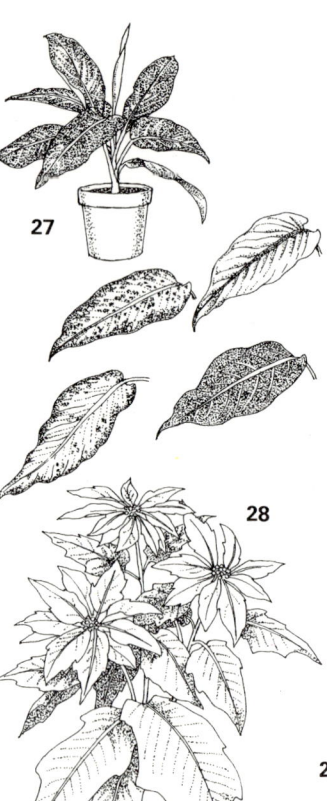

position and gradually reduce watering until they are dry. Start them off again in late summer in fresh compost after clearing away any dead matter. Place in a lighter aspect and begin watering again. Pests include aphids and thrips; grey mould and rot through poor culture may also affect them. Propagate by seeds sown in late summer to early autumn.

### 27 Dieffenbachia ●
Araceae
Dumb Cane
Most dieffenbachias available are varieties of *D. picta* which comes from Brazil. They are grown for their strikingly marked leaves, which may be 30 cm long. The plants themselves may grow from 45 cm to well over 1 m high. Though coming from tropical America they will put up with shade and in the summer should be shielded from direct sunlight. A humid atmosphere is best with a temperature preferably between 16 and 21°C. In winter avoid overwatering to prevent rot in cool conditions. Large plants can be grown by potting-on in JI 3, ending up in a 25- or 30-cm (10- or 12-in) pot. Generally free of pests and disease, but avoid rot as mentioned above. Propagate by stem cuttings placed in a mixture of equal parts of sharp sand and peat and kept at above 21°C.

**Dracaena** see **Cordyline**
**Echeveria** see **Succulents**
**Epiphyllum** see **Cacti**

## 28 Euphorbia
## pulcherrima ●●
Euphorbiaceae
Poinsettia
Once considered rather tricky
to maintain, modern strains,
such as the Mikkel-Rochford,
have overcome many of the
problems and are easier to
keep well clothed in leaves.
The flowers are small and
yellowish, but the plant is
grown for the brilliantly
coloured bracts which
surround them. Jl 2, light and
warmth, with a winter
temperature above 16°C, are
needed. After flowering they
may be dried off and started
again in the spring; some
people like to keep them
growing on. The plants like a
liquid feed about every two
weeks when growing from
spring to late autumn. Usually
fairly free of pests and disease.
Propagate in spring by cuttings
of young shoots about 10 cm
long. Dry off the latex sap
with paper tissue or powdered
charcoal before inserting, and
keep in a temperature of 18 to
21°C.

## 29 Exacum affine ●●
Gentianaceae
Persian Violet
A member of the gentian
family, the Persian Violet is a
native of the island of Socotra
in the Indian Ocean. It is
grown for its attractive violet-
blue flowers with yellow
centres. These smother the
plant from summer to winter
when it is grown well. Bushy
in appearance, it grows to
about 23 cm high. Jl 2 is a
suitable compost; it should be
kept moist and fed at about
two-week intervals when the
plant is growing. The

temperature should not fall
below about 16°C. Usually free
of pests and disease. An
annual, it will need raising from
seed sown in mid-spring, or
early autumn for larger plants,
if a minimum temperature of
about 16°C is maintained.

x **Fatshedera lizei** see
**Hedera**
**Faucaria** see **Succulents**

## 30 Ferns ●● – ●●●
Of the thousands of species, a
number of ferns make good
house plants. Most require
shade and moisture and a
compost rich in leaf mould or
peat. Such ferns, grown in
pots, include *Adiantum
capillus-veneris*, Maidenhair
Fern (30a), which has graceful
fronds and grows to about
25 cm high; *Asplenium
bulbiferum*, Hen and Chicken
Fern (30b), so called because
of the young plants which
form from small bulbs on the
fronds, grows to about 60 cm
high; and the related species
*A. nidus*, Bird's Nest Fern,
which looks rather like a large,
green shuttlecock, the fronds

growing to more than 1 m; it
requires warmer conditions.
*Blechnum capense* grows up
to 1 m; *Pteris ensiformis*
'Victoriae', Silver Table Fern
(30c), has graceful fronds, up
to 38 cm with silvery markings.
*Platycerium bifurcatum*, Stag's-
horn Fern (30d), however,
needs about half of its compost
to be sphagnum moss. This
plant may be grown in a pot,
in a hanging basket or on
bark. When grown on bark, the
roots should be put in a
similar mixture, wrapped round
with more moss, and tied to
the bark. The fern should be
kept moist and warm but often
survives some neglect. Pests
include woodlice and root
mealy bugs. Generally disease-
free. Propagation is by spores;
by plantlets in the case of
*Asplenium bulbiferum*; by
removal of young plantlets
arising from the roots of
platycerium; and by division.

## 31 Ficus ●●
Moraceae
Fig
The fig family contains one of
the best known house plants,

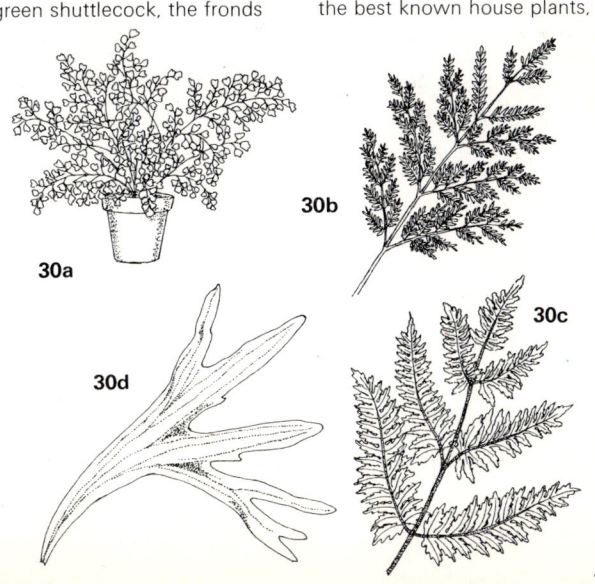

30a

30b

30c

30d

the Rubber Plant, *Ficus elastica*, as well as a number of other interesting species which are also good to keep. All require JI 2 or a soilless equivalent, well watered in summer, moist in winter, and a light position, preferably shaded from direct summer sunlight. Red spider mite, scale insects and mealy bugs are the main pests. Leaf loss and browning is probably due to cultural conditions— overwatering and draughts.

The best house plants are *F. elastica*, *F. pumila* and *F. radicans*, all very different from one another. *F. elastica* requires a temperature above

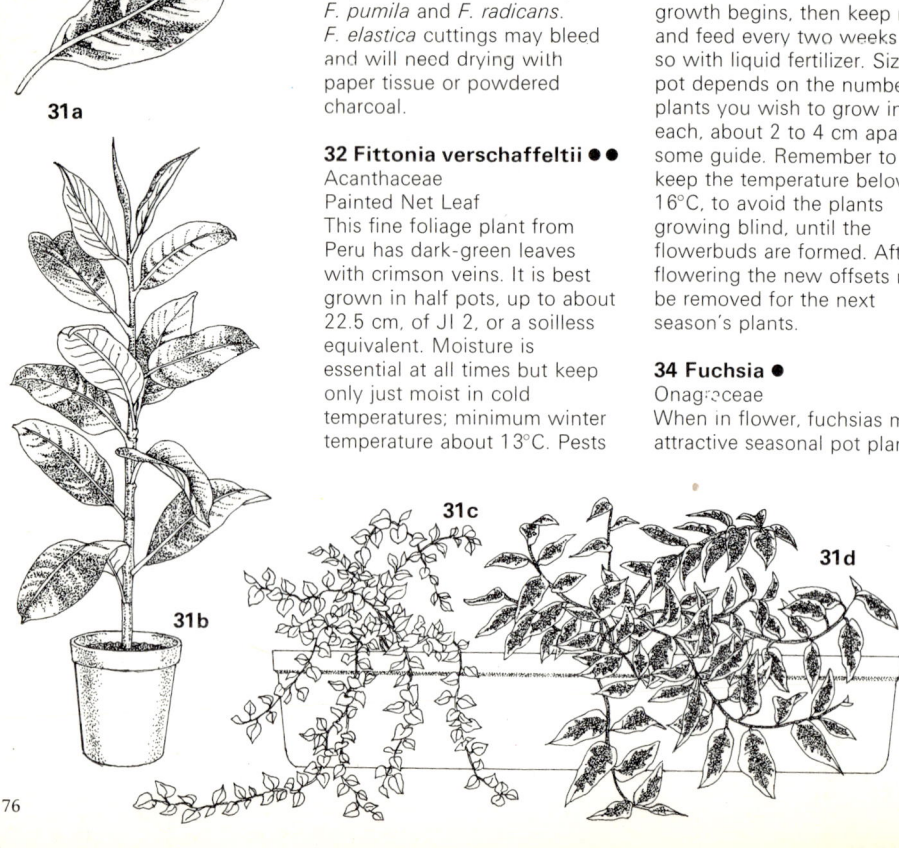

**31a**

**31b**

16°C in winter and may grow to ceiling height. It is best known in its varieties, 'Decora' (31a), green-leaved; 'Doescheri' (31b), variegated with white and pink; and 'Variegata', variegated cream and grey, sometimes flushed pink. *F. pumila*, Climbing Fig (31c), makes a good, trailing pot plant and has small green heart-shaped leaves closely set on the stems. It requires a temperature above 10°C in winter. *F. radicans*, Rooting Fig (31d), is most attractive in the variety 'Variegata', with cream-splashed leaves. It requires a temperature above about 13°C in winter. Excellent for trailing over a pot or basket. Propagate by cuttings, late spring to early summer, about 12 cm long for *F. elastica* and half as long for *F. pumila* and *F. radicans*. *F. elastica* cuttings may bleed and will need drying with paper tissue or powdered charcoal.

**32 Fittonia verschaffeltii ● ●**
Acanthaceae
Painted Net Leaf
This fine foliage plant from Peru has dark-green leaves with crimson veins. It is best grown in half pots, up to about 22.5 cm, of JI 2, or a soilless equivalent. Moisture is essential at all times but keep only just moist in cold temperatures; minimum winter temperature about 13°C. Pests

and disease usually infrequent. Propagate by division in mid-spring, starting the new plants in half pots of about 10 cm.

**33 Freesia × hybrida ●**
Iridaceae
Well known for its scented forms, the freesia is not an ideal house plant. It requires low temperatures until in bud and so grows better in a cold greenhouse or unheated conservatory. Freesias may be raised from seed sown in mid-spring to early summer in a cool place, or in the open in the early summer. They may also be raised from offsets in the late summer. Those started outdoors should be brought in in late autumn. JI 2 is a suitable compost. Do not keep more than just moist until growth begins, then keep moist and feed every two weeks or so with liquid fertilizer. Size of pot depends on the number of plants you wish to grow in each, about 2 to 4 cm apart is some guide. Remember to keep the temperature below 16°C, to avoid the plants growing blind, until the flowerbuds are formed. After flowering the new offsets may be removed for the next season's plants.

**34 Fuchsia ●**
Onagraceae
When in flower, fuchsias make attractive seasonal pot plants

**31c**

**31d**

but they are generally deciduous. There are now many hybrids. Usually they have two-colour flowers and vary in the length of their sepals and the inner and outer coloured parts of the flower. Some even have double petals. Others are suitable for laying down over pots or baskets. They should be grown in JI 3 or a soilless equivalent and kept moist when in growth. A cool position with full light, but not direct sunlight is also necessary. Young plants will need feeding every three weeks, increasing the frequency to every ten days or one week for established plants. Small plants will need 7.5-cm (3-in) pots but larger ones may require up to 30-cm (12-in) pots depending on the vigour of the variety. Repot in fresh compost annually in spring. Pests include whitefly and greenfly. Diseases are not common. Propagate by cuttings taken in mid-spring or late summer, about 8 cm long and rooted in a mixture of equal parts of peat and sharp sand. The temperature should be about 16°C.

Good varieties include: 'Arabella', white, rosy-red centre; 'Ballerina Mixed', for sowing, mixed colours; 'Cascade', for hanging pots or baskets, pink flushed white, crimson-red centre; 'Fiona', long white, rosy-mauve centre; 'Leonora', pink; 'Texas Longhorn', long red, white centre; 'White Spider', for hanging pots or baskets, white.

## 35 Gardenia jasminoides ●●●
Rubiaceae
Cape Jasmine
Well known for their heavily scented white to creamy-white flowers, gardenias come from the Far East—China and

Japan. They may grow several feet high and this must be borne in mind when positioning them, for they need plenty of light and humidity. Preferably, the temperature should remain between 16 and 24°C, or the buds will fail. They prefer an acid compost but JI 2 with regular feeds of sequestrene, or peat-based compost similarly treated, is suitable. Up to 20-cm (8-in) pots should be used: repot in early spring. The dark leaves are evergreen and the flowers, 7 to 10 cm across, appear during the summer. Buds may be pinched out after then. This improves the flowering strength by, in effect, giving the plants a rest for a few months. Pests include scale insects, mealy bugs and red spider mite.

Diseases are unlikely. Propagate by cuttings in early spring. The young shoots should be about 7 cm long with a head, planted in a mixture of equal parts of sharp sand and peat and kept at about 18°C.

**Gasteria** see **Succulents**
**Gloxinia** see **Sinningia**

## 36 Gynura ●
Compositae
Gynuras are evergreens mainly grown for the attractive forms in which leaves and stems are covered with purplish hairs, giving them a rather velvety appearance. They are members of the daisy family from India and Java. Keep moist for most of the year in plenty of light with some warmth. But in

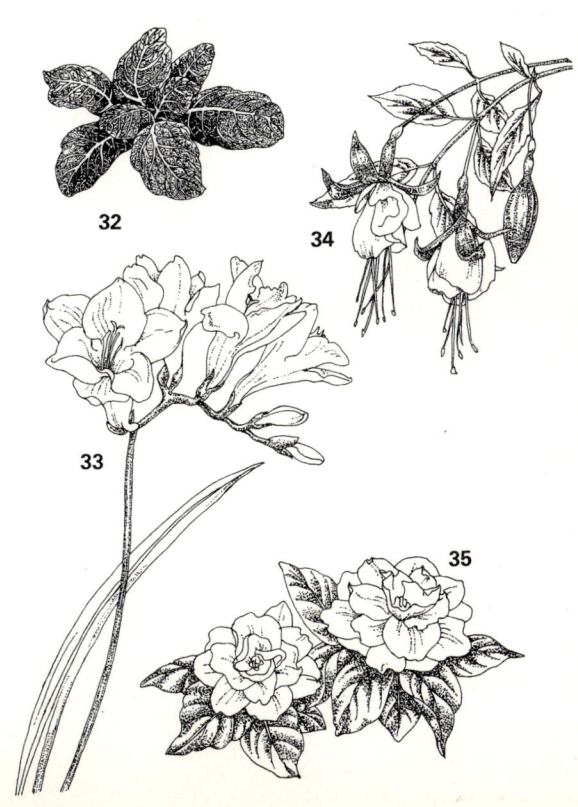

32

34

33

35

winter keep fairly dry and do not let the temperature fall below 13°C. JI 2, or a soilless equivalent, is suitable. Feed about every two weeks. Pinch out growing tips every so often to encourage bushiness, or leave to trail if growing *G. sarmentosa* in a hanging pot or basket. Repot in late spring and cut back side shoots to 5 or 7 cm in spring if growing for a second season. Generally free of pests and diseases. Propagate in spring by cuttings 6 to 7 cm long grown in a mixture of equal parts of sharp sand and peat and kept at 18°C.

**Haworthia attenuata** see **Succulents**

### 37 Hedera helix ●
Araliaceae
Ivy
These plants are suitable for cool and shaded positions and will survive some neglect. They may be trained up a support or left to hang down over their containers. JI 2, or a soilless equivalent, is suitable but they will grow in most mixtures kept just moist. The variegated forms will give better colour the more light there is, but sunlight is not necessary. A weak feed every two weeks or so is beneficial from spring to autumn. Repot into a larger pot if necessary, in spring. Pests are rarely troublesome, except possibly scale insect, and they are usually disease-free. Propagate by taking 10-cm tip cuttings in late summer. They will root in most composts, especially with the addition of a little sand.

Good varieties include: 'Buttercup', rich yellow leaves ageing to greenish; 'Cristata' (37a), light green, rounded with wavy edges; 'Glacier' (37b), silvery-green and white; 'Gold Heart' (37c), dark green with yellow centre; 'Sagittifolia' (37d) green, arrow shaped with a long often curved central lobe and 'Sagittifolia variegata' green, grey and white; 'Tricolor', green, grey and white, pink-flushed in autumn and winter x *Fatshedera lizei* (37e) is a hybrid with *Fatsia japonica* (37f). Sometimes known as the Ivy Tree, it grows upright to well over 2 m and may need supporting. It has large ivy-like leaves which in the form 'Variegata' have creamy margins.

### 38 Hibiscus rosa-sinensis ●●●
Malvaceae
Rose of China
This attractive Chinese shrub has given rise to many hybrids with brilliant flowers. The leaves, which remain evergreen if the winter temperature is constantly above 16°C, are usually medium to dark green; some varieties have cream variegations. The flowers may be single or double in yellow, orange, pink, red and crimson shades. The plants grow to about 2 m and need good light so limiting their potential indoors. JI 3, or a soilless equivalent, is suitable. Pot-on in mid-spring until a final pot size of 22.5 to 30 cm is reached. Feed every two to three weeks. Keep moist but only just if the winter temperature falls below 16°C, as the plants will shed leaves. The main pest is greenfly; generally disease-free. Propagate, from late spring to late summer, by 7-cm cuttings of side shoots with a head. Root them in a mixture of equal parts of sharp sand and peat and keep at 18°C. When

37a

37d

37c

37e

37b

37f

extending the flowering period from mid-winter to late spring. Flower colours are in shades of pink, rose, red, blue and yellow, or white. Plant in late summer or early autumn using pots or half pots of JI 2, or a soilless equivalent, for best results, or bulb fibre. The bulbs should be nearly touching and their tips exposed above the compost. Keep them moist, cool and dark until the flowerbuds are about 5 to 8 cm high, when they may be put into a lighter, but preferably still cool place, to flower. For growing in water see page 41. Pests and diseases are usually absent though rots may occur. Propagation by seeds or bulbs are lengthy processes to flowering size; fresh bulbs are usually bought annually.

### 41 Hydrangea hybrids ●
Hydrangaceae
Attractive flowering shrubs which make a colourful display when in flower but otherwise are not really good house plants. Being fairly hardy, they are usually able to spend the rest of the year outside, but of course, will need watering and care if kept in their pots. Flowers are white, rose-red and shades of pink, some varieties may be blued. Best to start with small bushy plants in late winter. Use JI 3, or a soilless equivalent, in 15- or 17.5-cm (6- or 7-in) pots kept at about 10°C. Water well and feed every two weeks when in full leaf. After flowering cut back and pot into larger pots for the next year. Usually fairly free of pests and diseases. Easy to propagate by cuttings, 10 to 13 cm long with about four leaves. Plant in moisture-retaining medium during late summer. When rooted start them off in 7.5- or 10-cm (3- or 4-in) pots and when

rooted pot into JI 2 using a 7.5-cm (3-in) pot. Young plants look best made to grow bushy by pinching out the growing tips until enough shoots have been started.

### 39 Hippeastrum hybrids ●
Amaryllidaceae
Usually sold as Amaryllis (a different plant), these hybrids are among the most magnificent flowering bulbs. Often they have huge trumpet flowers in shades of pink, red and crimson, sometimes striped with white or edged with another colour and white. The mid-green leaves are wide and star-shaped while the flowering stem—sometimes there is more than one per bulb—is stout and pale green and may reach 60 cm high. Specially prepared bulbs are available for flowering about Christmas but normally flowering is from

early spring onwards. Grow in 12.5- or 15-cm (5- or 6-in) pots of JI 2, or a soilless equivalent, with the top half of the bulb uncovered. The temperature should be about 16°C. Keep moist and feed every ten days or so. The leaves will go on growing after flowering but when they yellow gradually reduce watering until the leaves die. Keep dry until growth restarts. Usually fairly free of pests and diseases. Propagate by offsets or seed sown in spring and kept at 16 to 18°C.

### 40 Hyacinthus hybrids ●
Liliaceae
Hyacinth
These bulbs are not really suitable for growing in the house over several years. It is better to force new bulbs annually. Specially prepared bulbs are also available

another pair of leaves has formed pinch out the growing tip to make a bushy plant.

## 42 Hypocyrta glabra ●●
Gesneriaceae
This South American shrubby plant has curious, if not attractive, orange pouch-shaped flowers and dark green, glossy leaves (42a). It grows about 30 cm high, needs a temperature of 18 to 21°C and good humidity. JI 1, or a soilless equivalent, is suitable. Keep moist and prune away stems which have flowered. This encourages new shoots on which the flowerbuds form. Usually fairly free of pests and disease. Propagate by cuttings of new shoots.
(See page 79 for illustration.)

## 43 Impatiens ●
Balsaminaceae
Busy Lizzie (43a), *Impatiens wallerana* (also known as *I. holstii* and *I. sultani*), and Balsam (43b), *I. balsamina*, both make attractive pot plants, but the former is a perennial while Balsam is an annual. Both may be grown in 12.5- or 15-cm (5- or 6-in) pots using JI 1 or JI 2, or a soilless equivalent. Keep in a light position but preferably out of direct sunlight. During winter keep Busy Lizzie above 13°C. There are many strains of both plants in brilliant and pastel colours. Pests, in the form of greenfly, may be a nuisance. Leaf fall in winter is possibly due to too low a temperature. Propagate both by seeds sown in mid-spring and kept at about 16°C. When large enough start them off in 7.5- or 10-cm (3- or 4-in) pots and pinch out the growing point of the Busy Lizzie when a few leaves have formed. Busy Lizzie may also be propagated by cuttings taken from mid-

**43a**

**43b**

**44a**

**44b**

spring to mid-autumn in a mixture of equal parts of sharp sand and peat at about 16°C. When rooted treat as seed-sown plants.

## 44 Ipomoea ●
Convolvulaceae
Morning Glory
The Morning Glories are mostly derived from American species, mainly *Ipomoea violacea* (44a), which is also known as *I. tricolor* and *I. rubro-caerulea*, and *I. purpurea* (44b). Probably the most popular are the blue-flowered forms of *I. violacea* but other colours include pink, rose, red,

crimson, purple and blue striped with white. They grow to well over 2 m and so will need supporting. Grow annually from seed sown in mid-spring, after soaking for 24 hours, or 'chipping' the seed by filing a notch in the hard seed shell. When large enough transfer to 10- or 12.5-cm (4- or 5-in) pots of JI 1, or a soilless equivalent, and when these are full of root finally use a 20-cm (8-in) pot. They need plenty of light, warmth and water. The main pest is likely to be greenfly. Diseases are uncommon but whitening leaves may be due to too low temperatures, especially when young.

**Kalanchoe blossfeldiana** see **Succulents**

## 45 Lilium ●—●●
Liliaceae
Several lilies make quite good short-term house plants when they are in flower, while *Lilium formosanum* will survive several seasons. Keep moist when growing but with good drainage. JI 1 is suitable with broken crocks covering the bottom of a 17.5- to 20-cm (7- to 8-in) pot, or larger if more than one bulb. Half fill the pot with compost, place a layer of sand on top and then place the bulb in it. Cover the bulb with more compost mixed with sand. When growth is up to the top of the pot fill in the remaining area with compost. Water from the bottom and keep moist in a cool but light position. Pests include greenfly; rots and virus diseases may occur. Propagate by detaching scales, offsets and by seeds. Seeds of *L. formosanum* and *L. longiflorum* (45), Easter Lily, generally grow to flowering-size plants fairly quickly but other species

46a

46c

46b

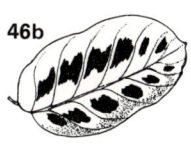

and hybrids may take some seasons. Those suitable include: *L. auratum*, Golden-ray Lily, and its varieties, having large flowers, white with yellow to reddish rays, fragrant, about 1 to 2 m; *L. formosanum*, white fragrant trumpets often flowering within one year from seed, 30 cm to 2 m; *L. longiflorum*, white, fragrant trumpets, 60 cm to 1 m; Mid-century hybrids, yellow, orange or red shades often with brownish speckles,

50 to 60 cm; *L. nepalense*, green, maroon-centred, fragrant, drooping flowers, 60 cm to 1 m; *L. speciosum* and its varieties, pink to crimson speckles on white to pink flushed ground, about 1 to 2 m.

**Lithops** see **Succulents**
**Mammillaria** see **Cacti**

### 46 Maranta leuconeura ●
Marantaceae
Prayer Plant, Rabbit's Tracks
This Brazilian plant has given rise to several spectacularly coloured foliage varieties. They are quick growers so, depending on the size you acquire, they are likely to require repotting fairly soon. The final pot size is usually about 15 cm (6 in) or a larger half pot. JI 2, or a soilless equivalent, is suitable. Keep moist and humid, feeding during summer to mid-autumn. Keep in shade with a winter temperature above 13°C. Pests and diseases usually absent. Propagate by dividing the root rhizomes in mid-spring. Cuttings may also be rooted from basal shoots during the summer. The varieties are: 'Erythrophylla', Red Herringbone Plant (46a), leaves marked with crimson veins and dark green blotches down the centre; 'Kerchoveana'

(46b), light veins on a grey-green leaf which has regular dark brown blotches down the centre, purple undersides; 'Massangeana' (46c), Rabbit's Foot, dark-green centred with white veins on smaller leaves.

### 47 Monstera ● ●
Araceae
Ceriman
Mexican and tropical American plants related to the common ivy. The two cerimans usually available as house plants are *Monstera deliciosa* (47), Mexican Bread Fruit, very tall growing, with large leaves, and *M. pertusa*, which has also been known as *M. deliciosa* 'Borsigiana' and is a more compact, and hence rather more suitable, house plant. They are also called Swiss Cheese Plants and grown for their leaves which are holed and slashed in irregular patterns. Large pots about 30 cm (12 in) with a compost such as JI 1 or 2, or a soilless equivalent, humidity and a winter temperature above 10°C are needed. Shade from direct sunlight in summer but too much shade will prevent the leaves developing. Feed every two weeks from mid-spring to early autumn. Usually free of pests and diseases, ill-looking leaves probably being due to poor watering. Propagate in

45

47

48

49

81

mid-summer by cutting off the stem with the growing tip with a mature leaf. Root at 24°C.

## 48 Narcissus ●
Amaryllidaceae
Narcissus, Daffodil
Several varieties are suitable for short-term house growing. Bulbs may be planted in autumn and cultivated as for hyacinths. Good varieties include: 'Carlton', yellow, large-cupped; 'Cragford', white, red cup, bunch-flowered; 'Double Event', white and orange, double cup; 'Dutch Master', yellow trumpet daffodil; 'Fortune', yellow, orange cup, large-cupped; 'Geranium', cream, orange-red cup, bunch-flowered; 'Grand Soleil d'Or', yellow flowers; 'La Riante', white, brilliant orange cup, small-cupped; 'Mount Hood', white, trumpet daffodil; 'Paperwhite Grandiflora', white bunch-flowered; 'Texas', yellow and orange, double.
(See page 81 for illustration.)

## Neoregelia see Bromeliads

## 49 Nerine ●●
Amaryllidaceae
South African plants related to the daffodil, they have large heads with many flowers mainly in pinks and reds.

**50**

According to the variety they grow from about 30 cm to 1 m and have daffodil-like leaves. Pot them individually in late summer in an 11.5-cm (4½-in) pot in JI 3, or a soilless equivalent, and cultivate as for *Hippeastrum*. They may remain in the same pots for about three seasons but require regular feeding when in leaf. Mealy bug is the main pest; yellow-blotched leaves are probably due to a virus disease. Propagate by offsets when repotting.
(See page 81 for illustration.)

## Nidularium see Bromeliads
## Opuntia see Cacti

## 50 Ornithogalum thyrsoides ●
Liliaceae
Chincherinchee
A member of the lily family from South Africa. The bulb flowers from late spring to early summer and grows up to 50 cm. Plant several bulbs in a 17.5-cm (7-in) pot in autumn using JI 2, or a soilless equivalent. Keep moist while growing and in a cool position. Usually free of pests and diseases. Propagate by offsets or seed sown in autumn.

## 51 Passiflora caerulea ●
Passifloraceae
Blue Passion Flower
A beautiful, vigorous climber from South America. Bought 'plants' are often made up of three cuttings giving a bushy appearance. They should be grown in JI 3, or a soilless equivalent, repotting as necessary until they are in about a 30-cm (12-in) pot. They need little feeding but plenty of light and water while growing. Keep just moist in winter at a temperature above 7°C. Usually fairly free of pests

**52a**

and diseases. Propagate by seed which germinates readily, or by 7-cm cuttings in late summer which when rooted pot into 7.5-cm (3-in) pots.

## 52 Pelargonium ●
Geraniaceae
Geranium
Four main types of geranium are grown as house plants: 1, scented leaf; 2, climbing; 3, regal; 4, zonal.
1 Scented-leaf geraniums. These have leaves of various shapes which have a scent when pressed. They include *Pelargonium crispum* and its variegated form (52a) in which the small, curled, fan-shaped leaves have creamy markings and a balmy scent; *P.* x *fragrans*, Nutmeg Geranium, has small hairy, heart-shaped leaves and a nutmeg scent; *P. odoratissimum*, Apple Geranium, has small, waxy leaves with an apple scent; *P. tormentosum*, Peppermint Geranium, is a rather sprawling plant with softly-haired, peppermint-scented leaves.
2 Climbing geraniums. Also known as ivy-leaved geraniums. They are derived from *P. peltatum* and are really trailing plants which may be supported on a trellis to give the impression of climbing. There are several varieties

**52b**

**52c**

**52d**

including 'Irene Genie',
salmon, 'Irene Modesty', white,
'Lollipop', vermilion; 'King of
Denmark', nearly double pink,
faint zone; 'Mr Henry Cox',
rose, variegated yellow, pink
brown and green leaves; 'Red
Black Vesuvius', dwarf, red,
dark brownish-black leaves;
'Spitfire', red, white
variegated leaves. Good strains
for raising from seed include:
'Carefree', 'Del Greco' and
'Fleuriste', many of which are
available mixed or by colour.

Grow plants in 12.5-cm
(5-in) pots using JI 2, or a
soilless equivalent. Water well
while growing but keep barely
moist in winter when the
temperature should not fall
below 9°C. If grown-on for a
second season repot in the
spring. Usually new plants are
raised by cuttings taken in late
summer. The old plants are
then discarded as they tend
to become cumbersome. Pests
include whitefly. 'Black leg',
blackening of the stem base,
also affects the plants,
particularly the base of
cuttings. Propagate by tip
cuttings about 7 cm long. Use
seed compost and plant one to
a 7.5-cm (3-in) pot or more if
the pot is bigger. When rooted,
pot-on into compost with
fertilizer and before too much
growth pinch out the growing
tip. This will encourage
branching and may be
necessary a second time. Seeds
should be sown in early spring.

including 'La France', with
double mauve flowers and
darker flecks; 'L'Elegante',
pinkish flowers and cream and
pink variegated leaves; 'Sussex
Lace' (52b), lilac-pink flowers
and creamy-yellow veined
leaves.
3 Regal or Martha Washington
pelargoniums. These have
large crisp, toothed leaves.
They grow 30 to 60 cm high
and have large flowers often
edged or veined with another
colour. Varieties include
'Aztec', red with dark veins and
broad white edges; 'Black
Knight', dark purplish, with fine
white edges; 'Carisbrooke',
rose flecked with crimson;
'Doris Frith' (52c), white wavy
petals with carmine-flecked
flower centres; 'Grand Slam',
rosy red with darker shading in
flower centres; 'May Magic',
frilled, orange petals with paler
flower centres and edges;
'Nomad' white, wavy petals

with crimson flecks on the
upper surface.
4 Zonal pelargoniums. These
make good house plants and
may be placed outdoors in
summer. They are the most
brilliantly coloured and the
easiest of the geraniums; many
have very distinctive leaves
which give rise to the name
'zonal' (52d). They vary from
dwarf types 15 cm high to
plants of 2 m. Some also have
variegated leaves. Various zonal
strains are now available for
raising plants from seed,
besides the popular varieties
sold in pots. Good varieties
include: 'A Happy Thought',
cerise, green leaves with large,
central, yellow splash; 'Caroline
Schmidt', red, variegated
leaves; 'Gazelle', salmon, free-
flowering, brownish zone on
leaves; 'Gustav Emich', orange,
faint zone on leaves; 'Irene',
an American strain in various
colours, tall-growing plants

**53a**　　　**53b**　　　**53c**　　　**53d**　　　**53e**

### 53 Peperomia ●
Piperaceae
Several species of these South and tropical American plants make popular house plants and are also used in bottle gardens. They are grown for their foliage rather than their plantain-like flowers. Use 9- or 10-cm (3½- or 4-in) pots with JI 1 or a soilless equivalent. Keep just moist while growing but almost dry in winter, when the temperature should not fall below about 10°C. They like plenty of light but not too much direct, scorching sun as they prefer a humid atmosphere. Repot into fresh compost every year in mid-spring. Usually free of pests and diseases. Propagate by cuttings from spring to late summer and, in the case of *Peperomia argyreia* (53a), also by leaf cuttings.

The main species grown in homes are: *P. argyreia*, up to 23 cm high and across, silvery leaves with darker green along the main veins; *P. caperata* (53b) and varieties, 10 to 23 cm high and across, dark-green, heavily corrugated leaves, the veins being sunken; *P. griseo-argentea* (53c), also known as *P. hederifolia*, similar to *P. caperata* but with larger, lighter greyish-green leaves and less sunken veins; *P. obtusifolia* (53d), also known as *P. magnoliifolia*, up to 23 cm high and 30 cm across, dark green, purple edged leaves in the typical form, but some varieties have glossy or variegated leaves (53e).

### 54 Philodendron ●
Araceae
Several species of the South American philodendrons make interesting house plants but as most are climbers they are not all suitable for long-term

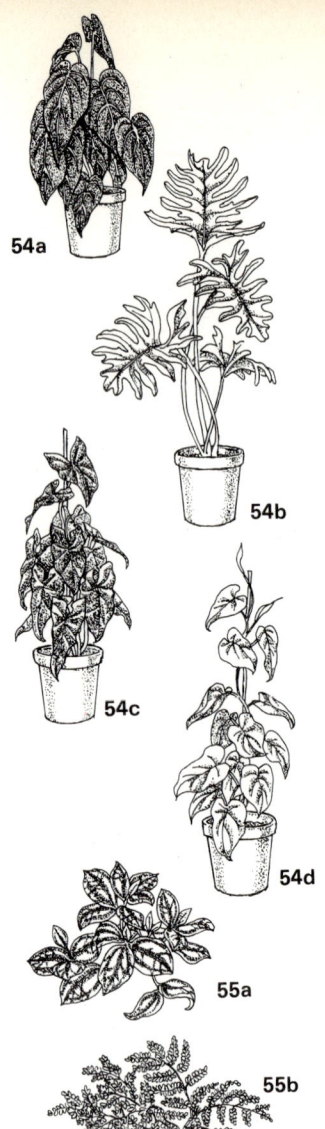

54a

54b

54c

54d

55a

55b

situations. Pot growing will provide some restriction, so if you have a conservatory or greenhouse, when you eventually plant them out they will exceed the heights given below. They are grown for their large and attractive leaves.

Use JI 1, or a soilless equivalent, and repot every other year, ending up with a pot size between 20 and 30 cm (8 and 10 in). Second-year plants need a little feeding in spring and summer. Keep moist at all times; which will mean more watering when the plants are growing and when the weather is warm. Humidity and good light, but not necessarily direct sunlight, are needed together with a winter temperature above 15°C. Pests usually absent but rotting may occur through overwatering especially in the winter.

Fine plants include: *Philodendron andreanum* (54a), often sold as *P. melanochryson*, dark brownish-green leaves with light veins, climbing to 2 m; *P. bipinnatifidum* (54b) has deeply cut and deep green leaves and does not climb but reaches about 1 m; *P. erubescens* (54c) climbs to 2 m or more, attractive rose-pink leaves when they emerge and which gradually darken to a glossy green, its variety 'Burgundy' is similar except that the young leaves are a shining bronze colour; *P. scandens* (54d) is probably the best known philodendron with weak climbing stems reaching 2 m or more which may be left to trail if not supported.

### 55 Pilea ●
Urticaceae
Members of the nettle family, two pileas make interesting house plants. *Pilea cadierei* (55a), Aluminium Plant, from the Far East, is grown for the aluminium green markings on its leaves and *P. microphylla* (55b), Artillery Plant, known also as *P. muscosa*, from tropical America. Both plants grow to about 23 to 30 cm, the Artillery Plant more bushy and

larger. Bushiness of the Aluminium Plant may be encouraged by pinching out the growing tips in spring. Plant in a 12.5- or 15-cm (5- or 6-in) pot using JI 2, or a soilless equivalent. They need good light, not direct sunlight, and a winter temperature of above 10°C. Keep moist at all times. Usually free of pests and diseases. Propagate by 7-cm cuttings, in late spring, and root them at 18°C or more.

**Platycerium** see **Ferns**

### 56 Polianthes tuberosa ●●●
Agavaceae
Tuberose
This Mexican plant has beautifully scented, white flowers but is not an easy house plant. It needs plenty of light and warmth with a winter temperature above 18°C to flower well. The tubers should be potted about 2 to 3 cm deep in JI 2, or a soilless equivalent, one per 12.5-cm (5-in) pot or several to a 17.5-cm (7-in) pot. The compost should be moist; watering is unnecessary until leaves appear when it must be kept moist. Pests and diseases are rare. Propagation is difficult and it is usual to replace the tubers every two or three years.

### 57 Primula ●
Primulaceae
Primrose
Useful plants for winter and spring flowering. The four main types of primrose grown as house plants are *Primula* x *kewensis* (57a), a hybrid with yellow, scented flowers and pale green leaves; and three Chinese species, *P. malacoides* (57b), Fairy Primrose, with flowers in shades of red, pink, lilac or white, and medium green leaves; *P. obconica*, with mauve, blue, carmine, red or

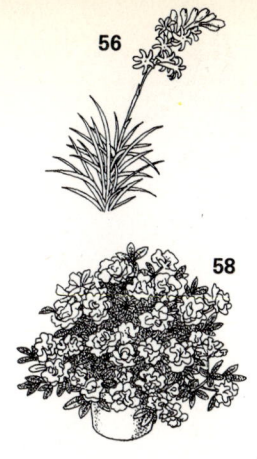
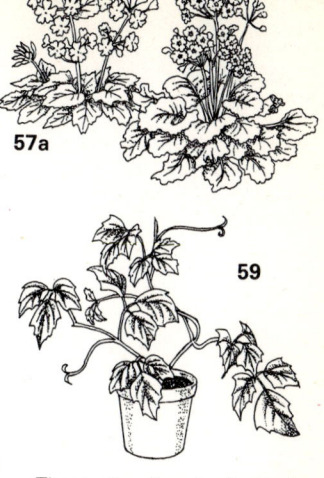

white flowers, and large, roundish leaves; *P. sinensis*, Chinese Primrose, with flowers in bright shades of red, pink and orange as well as purplish blues and white. Medium green leaves. Heights range from about 20 to 45 cm in the case of some Fairy Primroses. The leaves of some forms, particularly those of *P. obconica*, may cause unpleasant rashes for some people. Most primroses for the house are grown annually from seed. Sow in spring, or as soon as seed is available, and when ready start the individual plants off in 7.5- or 10-cm (3- or 4-in) pots of JI 2, or a soilless equivalent. Keep moist in a well lit position and feed regularly when the flowering stems start growing. Pot-on when necessary into 15-cm (6-in) pots. Greenfly and whitefly are common pests and moulds and rots frequent diseases, especially of seedlings.

**Pteris** see **Ferns**
**Rebutia** see **Cacti**
**Rhipsalidopsis** see **Cacti**

### 58 Rhododendron simsii ●●
Ericaceae
Indian Azalea

These attractive sturdy shrubs come from China. They are slow growing but reach about 1.5 m high. The flowers may be single or double in shades of crimson, red, pink or white. They appear in late spring or earlier if the plants are kept in the warm. The leaves are dark green. Use a lime-free compost in a 15-cm (6-in) pot for small plants and up to a 30-cm (12-in) pot for larger plants. Place in a cool position—a winter temperature of about 16°C is sufficient to induce winter flowering—and keep moist. A good indicator is the dark, moist bark at the base of the stem. If the zone is more than 1.5 cm high the plant is too wet, if less than 1 cm then it is too dry. Not usually troubled by pests and diseases. Propagate by seed—a slow process—or cuttings with a heel, in late summer or early autumn.

### 59 Rhoicissus rhomboidea ●
Vitaceae
Grape Ivy
Also known as *Cissus rhombifolia*, this is a fine climbing plant from South

**60**

**61**

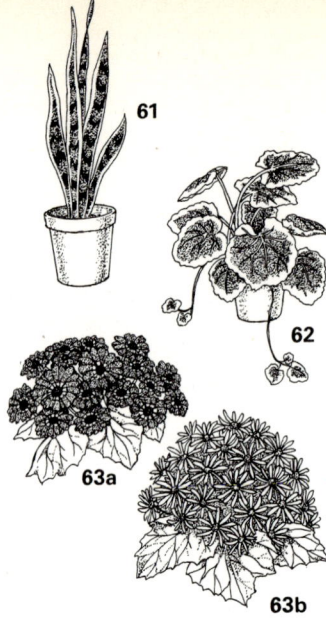

**62**

**63a**

**63b**

Africa. It has dark green leaves divided into three lozenge-shaped leaflets and usually grows to about 2 m. Start the plant off in a 15-cm (6-in) pot using JI 2, or a soilless equivalent, and repot annually in mid-spring, until in a 22.5-cm (9-in) pot. The plant will need supports as it climbs. It will tolerate some shade and needs a fairly cool position with a winter temperature above 10°C. Keep just moist at all times and feed from late spring to autumn. The leaves should occasionally be cleaned with water. Young plants should have the growing tips pinched out several times to encourage more climbing stems to develop. Usually fairly free of pests and diseases. Propagate by 7-cm cuttings in late spring and keep at about 18°C.

## 60 Saintpaulia ionantha ●●
Gesneriaceae
African Violet
A popular house plant from tropical Africa. It has dark green, velvety leaves and flowers in shades of violet, purple, pink or white with a yellow eye. It reaches about 10 cm high with a spread of 20 cm. Grow in a 10-cm (4-in) pot using a lime-free compost and repot every two years. Keep moist but not soaking and use water at about 15°C. Avoid splashing the leaves, which mark readily. Feed with a liquid fertilizer every fortnight from late spring to autumn. The plant also likes a humid atmosphere, a light

position out of direct sunlight and a temperature continually around 15°C. Fairly free of pests and diseases. Propagate in the summer by leaf cuttings kept at 18 to 21°C. Seed may be sown in spring.

## 61 Sansevieria trifasciata ●
Agavaceae
Mother-in-law's Tongue
A popular house plant from tropical Africa. The most usual form has stiff green and grey banded leaves up to about 50 cm; the variety 'Laurentii' is similar but with a yellow margin to the leaves while 'Hahnii' has squat, green leaves with yellow bands up to about 15 cm. Grow in 15-cm (6-in) pots using JI 2, or a soilless equivalent, and keep above 10°C in winter and 16°C at other times. A light, even sunny, position is needed and they should be kept fairly dry, especially in winter. Feed lightly in summer. Repot when pot bound. Pests and diseases are usually absent but

overwatering may cause rots of the roots and discoloured leaves. Propagate in summer by division of suckers or leaf cuttings.

## 62 Saxifraga stolonifera ●
Saxifragaceae
Mother of Thousands,
Strawberry Geranium
This Chinese saxifrage, also known as *Saxifraga sarmentosa*, is nearly hardy and thrives under the coolest of house conditions, putting up with a little shade too. It forms rosettes of rounded leaves, green with lighter veins and reddish undersides. Its variety 'Tricolor' has beautifully marked leaves with cream, pink and green predominating. Sprays of white flowers appear in summer. The plants, which grow up to about 25 cm, throw out runners with plantlets at the end and make it suitable for hanging pots or baskets. Grow in 15-cm (6-in) pots using JI 1. Keep just moist. Greenfly and whitefly may attack but pests and diseases are not common. Propagate by plantlets detached from the runners.

**Schlumbergera** see **Cacti**
**Sedum sieboldii** see **Succulents**

## 63 Senecio cruentus ●
Compositae
Cineraria
Also known as *Cineraria cruenta* and giving rise to many forms called *Senecio* 'Cruentus-hybrids' or *Cineraria* hybrids. These include *S. cruentus grandiflora* (63a) and *S. cruentus stellata* (63b). Despite the numerous names, growing them is fairly straightforward. They make small, bushy plants about 50 cm high topped with large flowerheads in many colours.

Start growing in a 10-cm (4-in) pot using JI 2 and pot-on to a final pot size of 15 or 20 cm (6 or 8 in). Initially keep the plants at 7°C, increasing the temperature to 16°C when the flowerbuds appear. After this feed regularly every two weeks and water carefully keeping the plants just moist. Shade from direct sunlight. Greenfly and whitefly may be a great nuisance. Overwatering can cause the plant to collapse. The best plants are raised annually from seed.

### 64 Sinningia hybrids ●
Gesneriaceae
Gloxinia
Mainly derived from the Brazilian *Sinningia speciosa* (64). During the summer gloxinias have rich, velvety trumpet flowers in a range of colours. The dark green, velvety leaves are almost stemless and form a rosette. They reach about 25 cm high and grow from tubers which, if bought, should be started in warm, moist peat, at about 21°C. When the plants are growing put them into 15-cm (6-in) pots of JI 2, or a soilless equivalent, and keep moist at 18°C. Feed at least every fortnight from when the flowerbuds appear until after flowering. Stop watering when the leaves die down, clear the tubers of dried growth and store in a dry place at about 13°C. Usually pest-free but various rots may occur. Besides dividing tubers in mid-spring

propagation is done by leaf cuttings, by cuttings of young shoots, with a small piece of tuber attached, and by seed.

### 65 Solanum capsicastrum ●
Solanaceae
Winter Cherry
A bushy annual shrub from Brazil grown for its brilliant red, cherry-shaped fruit in winter. Grows to about 50 cm high. Treat as for *Capsicum*.

### 66 Spathiphyllum wallisii ●●●
Araceae
White Sails
A South American plant (66a), this and the hybrid 'Mauna Loa' (66b) need warm conditions. Both have spearhead-shaped leaves on long stems and large, white spathes surrounding the yellowish flower spikes. *S. wallisii* grows about 20 to 40 cm high and 'Mauna Loa' up to 75 cm with larger spathes. Use JI 2, or a soilless equivalent, in 12.5- to 17.5-cm (5- to 7-in) pots. Repot annually in mid-spring. Keep moist, humid and warm. Feed every fortnight from spring to autumn, monthly in winter. Generally free of pests and diseases. Propagate by division in mid-spring.

### 67 Stephanotis floribunda ●●●
Asclepiadaceae
Madagascar Jasmine
This fragrant, white-flowered climber comes from

Madagascar. It is not a good house plant, needing a warm greenhouse and training against a wall or similar support. Small plants may be brought indoors to flower. Grow in 15-cm (6-in) pots with JI 2, or a soilless equivalent, and place in a light position at 18°C or more. Water well and keep a humid atmosphere. Feed every two weeks throughout the summer. Pests include scale insects and mealy bugs and incorrect cultivation may cause buds and leaves to fall. Propagate in mid-spring to early summer by 7-cm cuttings of unflowered side shoots, or by seed kept at about 24°C.

### 68 Succulents ●−●●
Succulents are a type of plant in which some or all of the parts have developed into water-storage organs. Cacti are succulents but as they form a large group they are treated separately. All succulents require fairly similar growing

67

64

65   66a   66b

conditions and those given earlier for the prickly cacti are generally suitable. Pests and diseases are also much the same. Propagation is usually by seed and in some types, such as the *Bryophyllum*, also by plantlets formed on the leaves and which may be detached and potted-up.

Popular plants include: *Aeonium* x *domesticum*, Crassulaceae; rather like a small bushy shrub with rosettes of leaves on the ends of the branches. It may reach 30 cm high and 60 cm across. Needs good light but not much heat.

*Agave* species, Agavaceae; mostly grow into very large plants with high flowering stems. Usually have long tapering leaves forming a rosette and often with variegated colours. *A. americana* 'Mediopicta' has green leaves with a band of yellow down the centre, grows to 1 m; *A. filifera*, Thread Agave, has bright green leaves edged white and grows to 25 cm; *A. victoriae-reginae*, dark green leaves with white lines and edges and a dark spine, grows to 37 cm.

*Aloe* species, Liliaceae; these include two easy house plants both of which produce similar spikes of tubular, dusty orange, flowers in summer. *A. aristata* forms a compact rosette of medium-green leaves with white raised spots and ending in a thread-like point, grows to 15 cm high and

18 cm across. Readily forms offsets. *A. variegata*, Partridge-breasted Aloe, forms rosettes of triangular, green leaves banded with white spots, grows to 23 cm high.

*Bryophyllum* species, Crassulaceae, often included with *Kalanchoe*, has two popular and rather different looking species both of which form plantlets on their leaves. *B. daigremontianum*, also known as *Kalanchoe daigremontiana*, grows to

75 cm, has pale blue-green leaves marked brownish red; *B. tubiflorum*, also known as *Kalanchoe tubiflora*, leaves of dusty green with brownish blotches, grows to 1 m.

*Crassula* species, Crassulaceae, form rosettes of fleshy leaves, need full sunlight but not heat, and should not be overwatered. *C. arborescens* has greyish-green leaves usually with a reddish margin, grows to 1 m. *C. falcata*, beautiful pale blue-green leaves, grows to 60 cm.

◀ Succulents comprise a wide range of plants which vary both in form and colour.
1 *Aeonium arboreum* 'Variegatum'
2 *Agave americana* 'Variegata'
3 *Aloe broomii*
4 *Aloe somaliensis*
5 *Bryophyllum tubiflorum*
6 *Crassula falcata*
7 *C. portulacea*
8 *Echeveria*
9 *E. derenbergii*
10 *E. multicaulis*
11 *Faucaria*
12 *Kalanchoe*
13 *Sedum morganianum*
14 *Stapelia*

*Echeveria* species, Crassulaceae, form rosettes of leaves with a waxy coating. *E. glauca*, has rosettes of bluish leaves, about 10 cm across, *E. harmsii*, also known as *Oliveranthus elegans*, has light green, hairy leaves in rosettes.

*Faucaria tigrina*, Aizoaceae, forms a nearly stemless cluster of eight to ten leaves, greyish green with lighter dots and edged with hooks rather like tigers' teeth, about 5 cm high.

*Gasteria maculata*, Liliaceae, has short, dark-green, strap-shaped leaves, with zig-zag whitish markings, arranged in two tiers, grows to 20 cm high.

*Haworthia attenuata*, Liliaceae, looks rather like a lighter green *Aloe aristata* but the rosette grows upwards as well, an easy house plant.

*Kalanchoe blossfeldiana*, Crassulaceae, grown for its often brilliantly coloured flowers in reds, oranges, yellows, pinks or white in winter. See also *Bryophyllum* above.

*Lithops* species, often known as Living Stones or Pebble Plants. These are mostly small plants 1 to 4 cm high, composed of a pair of thick

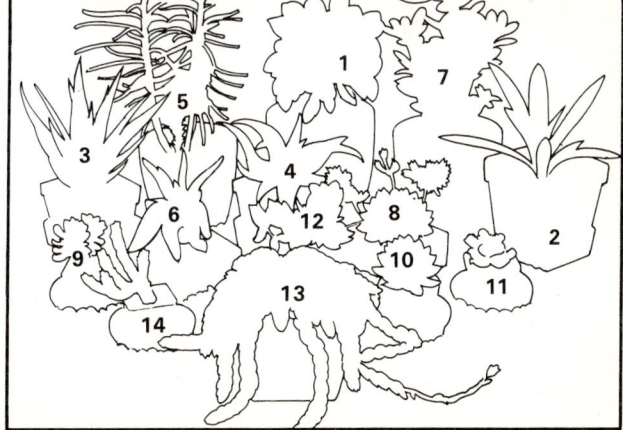

leaves joined except for a slit at the top from where the flower emerges. According to species the leaf colour varies through greys, browns and greens or even purplish.

*Sedum sieboldii*, Crassulaceae, is quite distinctive in its commonly available variety, 'Medio-variegatum'. Arching stems, 37 cm long, are surrounded by spirally arranged leaves, blue-green in colour, striped creamy white. Suitable for hanging pots or baskets.

*Stapelia* species, Asclepiadaceae, provide some plants with extremely unpleasantly scented flowers. *S. variegata* is the best known, with brownish, grey-green stems up to about 15 cm. Yellowish flowers in late summer, but variable.

## 69 Tetrastigma voinierianum •
Vitaceae
Related to, and somewhat similar to, Grape Ivy, *Rhoicissus rhomboidea*, this is a more vigorous plant with larger, lighter-green leaves, grey felted beneath. Treat it in the same way but keep the winter temperature above 13°C, and use a larger pot for the bigger plants.

## 70 Thunbergia •
Acanthaceae
Two South African species of thunbergia are usually available; the really hardy annual *T. elata* (70), Black-eyed Susan, orange flowers with a dark eye and *T. gregorii*, an orange-flowered perennial often incorrectly sold as *T. gibbsonii*. Both may climb to about 3 m, flowering from early summer to mid-autumn. Start in 7.5-cm (3-in) pots and pot-on to a 20- or 22.5-cm (8- or 9-in) pot, using JI 2, or

a soilless equivalent. They will tolerate sunny positions and need plenty of moisture while growing. *T. gregorii* should be kept just moist over winter in a temperature above 10°C. It may be pruned down to about 30 cm in early spring. Usually fairly free of pests and diseases. Propagate by seed sown in early spring.

## 71 Tolmiea menziesii •
Saxifragaceae
Pick-a-back Plant, Youth-on-age
From western USA. It grows about 20 cm high with a spread of 37 to 45 cm or more. The small, white and red dotted flowers are borne on spikes up to 60 cm high in early summer. Use JI 2, or a soilless equivalent, in 7.5-cm (3-in) pots for small plants and 17.5- or 20-cm (7- or 8-in) pots for the largest ones. Keep moist, but only just in winter, and feed every month or so. Being really hardy they may be placed in cool as well as sunny positions. Mostly free of pests and diseases. Propagate by detaching leaves with plantlets and potting them in 7.5-cm (3-in) pots.

## 72 Torenia fournieri •
Scrophulariaceae
Wishbone Flower
An annual plant from Indo-China with interesting flowers of pale lilac, with a violet 'wishbone', and a yellow blotch on the lower petal. A bushy plant, it grows about 30 cm high and flowers freely from mid-summer to autumn. Start in 7.5-cm (3-in) pots using JI 2, or a soilless equivalent, and pot-on up to about a 15-cm (6-in) pot. Pinch out the growing tips to encourage bushiness. Keep moist and sheltered from direct sunlight; it may be grown in a

cool or warm position. Usually fairly free of pests and diseases. Propagate by seed sown in mid-spring with a temperature about 18°C. 'Grandiflora' is a larger-flowered form and 'Alba' has white flowers.

## 73 Tradescantia and Zebrina ●
Commelinaceae
Two of the most common species are called Wandering Jew, *Tradescantia albiflora*, and *Zebrina pendula*. Speedy Jenny refers to *T. fluminensis*. All come from South America and have somewhat similar-shaped leaves, variously striped in the cultivated forms, and which fairly densely cover the straggly, fleshy stems. This makes them good for hanging or trailing. Start in 7.5-cm (3-in) pots using Jl 2, or a soilless equivalent, up to about a 15-cm (6-in) pot. Repot in mid-spring. Keep well watered while growing, just moist in winter when the temperature should be above 13°C. Feed every two weeks or so while growing and shade from direct sunlight. Fairly free of pests, browning and shrivelling leaves probably being due to incorrect watering. Propagate from late spring to late summer by detaching stem tips, 5 to 7 cm (2 to 3 in) long.

## 74 Tulipa ● ●
Liliaceae
Tulip
Short-term house plants, being more suited to growing in the garden, they may be used to provide colour in the house in late winter and early spring. Treat them as for hyacinths. Pests include greenfly and mice. Most other troubles are probably due to cultural conditions.

## 75 Vallota speciosa ●
Amaryllidaceae
Scarborough Lily
A most attractive bulb from South Africa, also known as *Vallota purpurea*. It is rather like a smaller-flowered *Hippeastrum*, to which it is related. The three or four trumpet-shaped flowers are a purplish-tinged bright red. The flower stem may be 50 to 60 cm high towering above the arched, green, strap-shaped leaves. Treat as for *Hippeastrum*, except that it does not require drying off, as it grows throughout the year.

**Vriesea splendens** see **Bromeliads**
**Zebrina** see **Tradescantia**

# Con-version tables

The metric system of measurement has been used throughout this book. The figures below give approximate equivalents in the imperial system.

**Length**
1 cm = $\frac{4}{10}$ in
2.5 cm = 1 in
10 cm = 4 in
15 cm = 6 in

20 cm = 8 in
30 cm = 1 ft
45 cm = 1 ft 6 in
60 cm = 2 ft
90 cm = 3 ft
100 cm = 3 ft 3 in
(1 m)      (about 1 yd)

**Temperature**
To convert temperatures from °C to °F use the following formula:

$$°C \times \tfrac{9}{5} + 32 = °F$$

Useful equivalents are (approximately):
4°C = 40°F
10°C = 50°F
13°C = 55°F
16°C = 60°F
20°C = 68°F
21°C = 70°F
24°C = 75°F
25°C = 77°F
26°C = 80°F

# Book list

Useful books and magazines, for further reading on house plants, may be divided into five main categories. First, those which are concerned only with house or indoor plants; they are often well illustrated encyclopedias of their subject and are the nearest extensions to the Guideline. Among them are:

**The Complete Book of Houseplants and Indoor Gardening,** prepared in association with the House of Rochford, Octopus, 1976. £4.95.

**The Complete Indoor Gardener,** edited by Michael Wright, Pan, 1974. Hardback £6, paperback £3.95.

Second, the A-Z dictionary type, heavily illustrated, with general cultural hints and brief descriptions of a large number of plants. They include:

**The ABC of House and Conservatory Plants,** Jocelyn Baines and Katherine Key, Michael Joseph, 1973. £4.50.

**The Dictionary of Indoor Plants in colour,** Roy Hay, F. R. McQuown, G. and K. Beckett, published in collaboration with the Royal Horticultural Society by Ebury Press and Michael Joseph, 1974. £6.

Third, general books on plants including house plants. The reader will often need to know the name of the plant he is looking for. Two such are:

**The Reader's Digest Encyclopaedia of Garden Plants and Flowers,** consultant editor Roy Hay, 1971, a compact but most informative book; and the weighty, four volume plus supplementary volume, Royal Horticultural Society's **Dictionary of Gardening.**

The fourth group covers a wide range of books, varying in price and quality. Some are heavily illustrated with eye-catching photographs, but are of little practical use, and others are illustrated with whimsical line drawings. Certainly buy if they take your fancy, but they are unlikely to be of as much use as those named above.

Fifth, magazines, and sometimes newspapers, carry useful articles. **The Garden, Amateur Gardening** and **Garden News,** although entirely different in their approach, have in their own manner interesting articles on house plants.

# Societies

Besides local garden clubs and societies, there are several important national organizations. The Royal Horticultural Society, Vincent Square, London SW1P 2PE, is of outstanding value. Although it embraces all aspects of gardening, its monthly journal called **The Garden,** and its regular shows, as well as its gardens and greenhouses at Wisley, usually have features of interest throughout the year. Specialist societies include the following:

**British Fuchsia Society,** Secretary, R. Ewart, 20 Bratton Avenue, Devizes, Wiltshire

**British & European Geranium Society,** Secretary, A. Biggin, Morval, The Hills, Bradwell, Sheffield, S30 2HZ

**British Pelargonium & Geranium Society,** 129 Aylesford Avenue, Beckenham, Kent BR3 3RX

**British Pteridological (Fern) Society,** Secretary, J. W. Dyce, Hilltop, 46 Sedley Rise, Loughton, Essex

**National Begonia Society,** Secretary, A. D. Potty, 36 Norton Avenue, Tolworth, Surrey

**Nerine Society,** Secretary, C. A. Norris, Brookend House, Welland, Worcestershire

**Saintpaulia and Houseplant Society,** Secretary, Miss N. Tanburn, 82 Rossmore Court, Park Road, London NW1

# Suppliers etc.

There are not many retail outlets specializing in house plants but a good florist will be able to supply the more unusual and tender plants; while most general nurseries sell the hardier types. It could also be well worthwhile getting in touch with your local garden society or club. Specialists will usually be found advertising their wares in the gardening press.

# Common name index

Words in italics following the popular name give the botanical name. Numbers in italics refer to illustrations.

# Index

# Credits

**Artists**
Ron Hayward Art Group
Anne Isseyegh
B. L. Kearley Ltd
QED
John Shackell
Temple Art Agency

**Photographs**
A-Z Collection: 5
Heather Angel: 49
Mary Evans: 6, 7
Paul Forrester: 37
Marshall Cavendish: 18
Giuseppe Mazza: 73
Pan Britannica Industries: 23
House of Rochford/ADA, 2, 30
John Sims: 5 (inset), 17, 31,
  68–9, 88
Harry Smith Collection: 19
Elizabeth Whiting: 27, 57

**Cover**
Design: Design Machine
Photograph: Paul Forrester